SERIES EDITOR: **Roger Porkess**

Formula One
MATHS Gold

C

Susan Ball ● **Dave Blackman**

Margaret Bland ● **Sophie Goldie**

Abigail Kent ● **Katie Porkess**

Susan Terry ● **Leonie Turner**

Brandon Wilshaw ●

Hodder & Stoughton

A MEMBER OF THE HODDER HEADLINE GROUP

Acknowledgements

The authors and the publishers would like to thank the following companies, agencies and individuals who have given permission to reproduce copyright material. Every effort has been made to trace and acknowledge ownership of copyright. The publishers will be glad to make suitable arrangements with any copyright holder whom it has not been possible to contact.

Illustrations were drawn by Maggie Brand, Jeff Edwards, Claire Philpott

Photos supplied by
page 24 © R D Battersby/TOGRAFOX
page 57 © WildCountry/CORBIS
page 58 © CORBIS
page 70 © Francesc Muntada/CORBIS
page 153 © Jeremy Horner/CORBIS
page 168 © Chris Lisle/CORBIS
page 175 © Kevin Schafer/CORBIS

Cover design and page design by Julie Martin.

Orders: please contact Bookpoint Ltd, 130 Milton Park, Abingdon, Oxon
OX14 4SB. Telephone: (44) 01235 827720.
Fax: (44) 01235 400454. Lines are open from 9.00–6.00, Monday to Saturday, with a
24-hour message answering service.
You can also order through our website www.madaboutbooks.co.uk.

British Library Cataloguing in Publication Data
A catalogue record for this title is available from The British Library

ISBN 0 340 869348

First published 2004
Impression number   10 9 8 7 6 5 4 3 2 1
Year   2010 2009 2008 2007 2006 2005 2004

Copyright © 2004 Susan Ball, Dave Blackman, Margaret Bland, Sophie Goldie, Abigail Kent, Katie Porkess, Roger Porkess, Susan Terry, Leonie Turner, Brandon Wilshaw

Cover photo from Jacey, Debut Art

Typeset by Tech-Set Ltd, Gateshead, Tyne & Wear
Printed in Italy for Hodder & Stoughton Educational, a division of Hodder Headline Plc, 338 Euston Road, London NW1 3BH

Introduction

This book is designed for Year 9 students working at Levels 3 to 5 of the National Curriculum, and is accompanied by a substantial Teacher's Resource. Preceding books cover Years 7 and 8. These three *Gold* books are an integral part of the *Formula One Maths* series and may be used alongside books A1, B1 and C1 during the three years of Key Stage 3.

The series builds on the National Numeracy Strategy in primary schools and its extension into Key Stage 3. It is designed to support that style of teaching and the lesson framework.

This book is presented as a series of double-page spreads, each of which is designed to be a lesson. The left-hand page covers the material to be taught and the right-hand page provides questions and activities for the students to work through. Each chapter ends with a 'Finishing off' review exercise covering all its content. Further worksheets, tests and ICT materials are provided in the Teacher's Resource.

In addition there are three 'reward' lessons. These contain questions which on the one hand lead to the solution of a puzzle and on the other provide valuable revision. These lessons are for use when students have completed a period of hard work.

A key feature of the left-hand pages of lesson spreads is the tasks. These are the main teaching activity for the lesson, and provide opportunities for students to work singly, in pairs, groups, or as a class. The tasks use the students' own experiences to reinforce the teaching for that particular lesson; many of them are based around everyday life. Each of the tasks is supported by a photocopiable task sheet in the Teacher's Resource; these are designed to ensure the time is spent on maths, not on copying out tables and graphs, and to enable students to build up a body of work that they can be proud of.

The left-hand pages include many discussion points. These are designed to help teachers engage their students in whole class discussion. Teachers should see the ? icon as an opportunity and an invitation.

The last part of each lesson is the plenary. The teacher and students discuss what they have been doing and the mathematics involved. This is usually supported by discussion points in the Student's Book, and by quite extensive advice in the Teacher's Resource. The Teacher's Resource also includes lesson objectives, and the plenary is the time to check that these have been met.

The various icons and instructions used in this book are explained overleaf.

The order of the chapters ensures that the subject is developed logically, at each stage building on previous knowledge; there are many review spreads reminding students of earlier work. Chapter 24 consists entirely of revision questions to help with preparation for the Key Stage 3 National Test. The final two chapters are designed to be done between the National Test and the end of term. The Teacher's Resource includes a scheme of work based on this order. However, teachers are of course free to vary the order to meet their own circumstances and needs.

This series stems from a partnership between Hodder and Stoughton Educational and Mathematics in Education and Industry (MEI).

The authors would like to thank all those who helped in preparing this book, particularly those involved with writing materials for the accompanying Teacher's Resource.

Roger Porkess   2004
Series Editor

How to use this book

 You will have a discussion about this point with your teacher and the rest of the class.

 Use your calculator for this question.

 You are not allowed to use your calculator for this question.

 Your teacher may give you a sheet to write on. This will save time copying out tables and graphs.

 Warning. This is a common mistake. Or, take extra care over this question.

 There is some ICT material in the Teacher's Resource for this work.

This book is a series of double-page spreads. The left-hand page is the teaching page. The right-hand page gives exercise questions, activities or investigations on the topic.

You will also come across the following features.

This is the main activity of the lesson. You are expected to spend quite a lot of time on it. It will help you understand the work. Ask your teacher if you need help.

 Do the right thing!

You are learning something practical. Here are step-by-step instructions to follow.

Contents

Metric units review

? How many grams (g) are there in a kilogram (kg)?

How much does it cost to send this parcel?

First class - Fragile

Weight	Cost
up to 0.25 kg	£1.10
0.5 kg	£1.45
0.75 kg	£2.05
1.0 kg	£2.80
1.5 kg	£3.70
2 kg	£4.35
3 kg	£5.75
Over 3 kg, £5.75 + 99p for every extra 200 g or part of 200 g	

Task

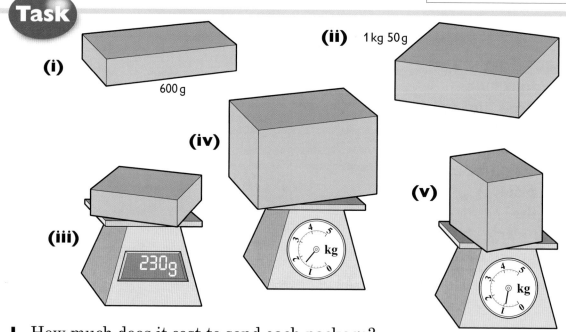

(i) 600 g

(ii) 1 kg 50 g

(iii) 230g

(iv)

(v)

1 How much does it cost to send each package?

2 All the packages are then wrapped together in one very large parcel.
   (a) How much does it cost to send them in this way?
   (b) How much does this save?

3 Put the packages together into two big parcels.
   How much does each parcel cost to post?

4 Find the cheapest way of posting the packages in two big parcels.

? What is the heaviest parcel that can be sent for £10?

Exercise

Use the most suitable units to answer these questions.
This table of metric units will help you.

Length	Weight	Capacity/volume
10 mm = 1 cm	1000 g = 1 kg	10 ml = 1 cl
100 cm = 1 m	1000 kg = 1 tonne	100 cl = 1 litre
1000 mm = 1 m		1000 ml = 1 litre
1000 m = 1 km		

1 A fence has 100 posts, each 1.75 m long.
What is the total length of the posts?

All sides are the same length.

2 What is the perimeter of the pentagon?

250 cm

3 The perimeter of a square is 1 km.
What is the length of one side?

4 The length of Sam's pace is 60 cm.
How far does she walk in 100 paces?

5 The recipe makes pancakes for 3 people.

(a) Write it out to make enough pancakes
for 30 people.

(b) Write the amount of milk in litres.

(c) There are 6 eggs in a box.
How many boxes of eggs are needed?

(d) Look at the weighing scales.
How much more flour is needed?

(e) Look at the two measuring jugs.
How much more milk is needed?

Pancake recipe
Ingredients for 3 people

1 egg
125 g flour
250 ml milk
pinch of salt

2 litres
$1\frac{1}{2}$
1
$\frac{1}{2}$
Milk

1000 ml
750
500
250

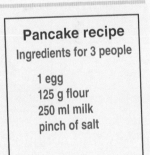

Flour

150g

Imperial units review

Mrs Patel is filling out Class 9G's medical cards.

I am 50 inches tall.

Sophie

? How tall is Sophie in feet and inches?

 Task

12 inches = 1 foot
14 pounds = 1 stone

I am 6 ft 1 in tall.
I am 15 lb heavier than Lucy.

Pete

I am 1 ft shorter than Karl. I weigh 5 lb more than Mercy.

Ali

I am 2 in taller than Ali and 10 in shorter than Karl. I weigh 7 st 10 lb.

Mercy

I am 3 in shorter than Pete. This is my weight.

Karl

I am 2 in shorter than Karl. This is my weight.

Lucy

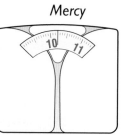

Copy and complete this table, using the information from the diagram.

Name	Weight in pounds	Weight in stones and pounds	Height in inches	Height in feet and inches
Ali				
Karl				
Lucy				
Mercy				
Pete				

? What other imperial units are there?
Why has the UK changed to the metric system?

Exercise

This is a table of imperial measures.

Length	Weight	Volume/Capacity
12 inches (in) = 1 foot	16 ounces (oz) = 1 pound	8 pints (pt) = 1 gallon
3 feet (ft) = 1 yard	14 pounds (lb) = 1 stone	
1760 yards = 1 mile	2240 pounds = 1 ton	

1 Use the table of measurements to change these lengths to yards.

(a) 10 feet (b) 15 feet (c) 24 feet

(d) 144 inches (e) $\frac{1}{4}$ of a mile

2 Change these measurements to feet.

(a) 6 yards 1 foot (b) 9 yards 2 feet

(c) 12 yards (d) 25 yards

3 Mrs Black runs a small hotel.
This is her milk order for one week.
Copy the table and fill in the missing numbers.

	Sun	Mon	Tues	Wed	Thurs	Fri	Sat	Total
Pints	10		14		8			
Gallons	$1\frac{1}{4}$	2		$1\frac{3}{4}$		$\frac{3}{4}$	$1\frac{3}{4}$	

4 Imperial measures are still used in some sports events.
Match the correct measurement to each picture.

26 miles 385 yards   22 yards   250 yards

Time

Mum's flight is late.

Arrivals			Time: 1125
Flight no.	**From**	**Due at**	**Comment**
EZY611	Heathrow	1940	Landed 2004
BA1184	Stansted	2215	Landed 2305
AF163	Aberdeen	2335	Delayed 45 min
BY261	London	0025	Expected 0015
EZT621	Alicante	0040	On time

? Mrs Smith's flight from Aberdeen is late.
What time is it expected to land?

? How much longer do they have to wait?

Task

This is the airport's Information Board for the same day.
Some details are missing.

Flight no.	From	Departure	Flight time	Arrival	Comment	Expected
T4023	Aberdeen	2106	45 min	2151	On time	
BA7134	Gatwick	2133		2228	On time	2228
EZY8334	Malaga	2148	3 h 20 min			0108
KL194	Madrid		1 h 50 min	2355	20 min late	0015
BE229	Luton	2210	40 min			2307
AF2226	Paris		1 h 35 min		25 min late	2325
EZY4537	Prague	2244	3 h 15 min		On time	
BA7137	Heathrow		50 min	0045	On time	0045

I Which flight leaves at ten past ten in the evening?
2 Which flight is expected to arrive at a quarter past midnight?
3 Copy the table and complete the missing information.

? A flight from London to New York takes 7 hours.
It leaves London at 0900 and arrives in New York at 1100.
Explain this.

Exercise

1 Write the 24-hour times for these clocks.

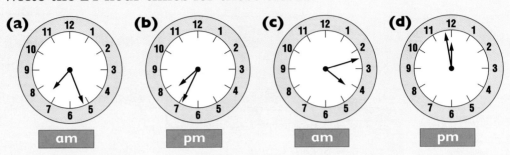

(a) am   **(b)** pm   **(c)** am   **(d)** pm

(i) Which clock is just after half past seven?

(ii) Is clock **(d)** just before midday or just before midnight?

(iii) What will you be doing tomorrow at the time shown on clock **(c)**?

2 Use a calculator to change these times to minutes.

(a) 2 hours   **(b)** $1\frac{1}{2}$ hours   **(c)** 3 hours 20 minutes

(d) 5 hours   **(e)** $4\frac{1}{4}$ hours   **(f)** 2 hours 30 minutes

3 **(a)** Write down this time.

(b) Write the time it will be in
   (i) 10 minutes
   (ii) 100 minutes.

4 **(a)** Using today's date, find the ages of these people in years and months.

(b) How many days older is
   (i) Ahmed than Rich
   (ii) Karen than Ahmed?

Name	Date of birth
Rich	24–05–1982
Karen	08–09–1979
Ahmed	17–10–1981

5 What is the length of each programme in this TV guide?

Programmes

12.20	**Football preview**
1.00	**News; Weather**
1.25	**Racing** from Sedgefield
2.35	**World snooker**
3.45	**Half-hour football roundup**

Speed

We have gone 100 miles in 2 hours. How fast is that?

100 miles in 2 hours, is $\frac{100}{2} = 50$ miles in 1 hour, so our speed is 50 mph.

Speed = Distance ÷ Time
Distance = Speed × Time
Time = Distance ÷ Speed

Task

This map shows where some students live.

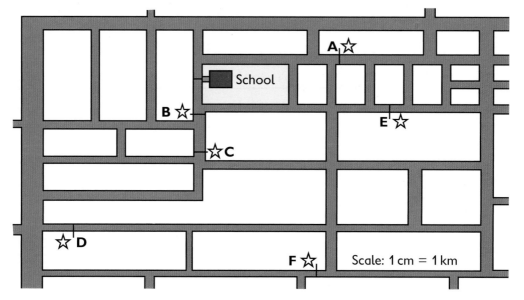

Scale: 1 cm = 1 km

The table below gives details of their journeys to school.

Person	Distance (nearest km)	Travel	Time (min)	Speed (km per hour)	Lives at ☆
Jack	10	Bus	30		
Kim	9	Car	15		
Tim	1	Bike		12	
Mark	2	Walk		6	
Megan		Bike	15	16	
Michelle		Car	10	36	

Copy and complete the table.

What are the standard speed restrictions on our roads?

What types of roads do they apply to?

Exercise

1 A jogger runs at a steady speed of 12 kilometres per hour.
A walker walks at a steady speed of 6 kilometres per hour.
Copy and complete this table to show how far they travel.

	$\frac{1}{4}$ hour	20 min	45 min	1 hr	$1\frac{1}{2}$ hr	2 hr
Jogger				12 km		
Walker				6 km		

2 The distances between the villages is shown in the table.

	Norton	Bishopton	Thorpe	Carlton
Norton		5 km	7 km	5 km
Bishopton	5 km		4 km	6 km
Thorpe	7 km	4 km		3 km
Carlton	5 km	6 km	3 km	

Sophie walks at 6 km per hour.
How long do these walks take her?

(a) Carlton to Bishopton

(b) Carlton to Thorpe

(c) Norton to Thorpe to Carlton

(d) Bishopton to Thorpe to Carlton

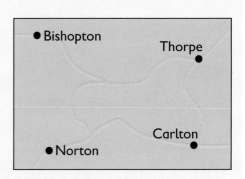

3 Copy the table and use the speedometer to complete it.

Miles per hour	Kilometres per hour
30	
	80
	95
70	

5 miles = 8 kilometres

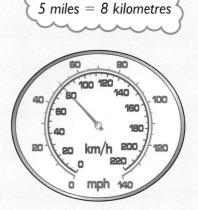

Finishing off

Now that you have finished this chapter you should be able to:

- use everyday units of length, weight, volume (or capacity) and time
- convert one metric unit to another
- convert one imperial unit to another.

Review exercise

1   This bus is measured in millimetres.
- Length   10 000 mm
- Width   2500 mm
- Height   4300 mm

(a) How long is the bus in metres?

(b) Does the bus fit under the bridge?

(c) How much clearance is there on either side of the bus?

2   Jo, Samir, Kim, Mercy, John and Becky went fishing. Here are their biggest fish.

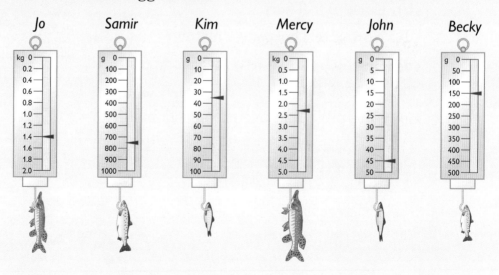

(a) Write the weights of the fish in order, the smallest first.

(b) What is the total weight of the fish on Samir's, Kim's and Becky's scales?

(c) Is Mercy's fish heavier than all the other fish weighed together?

SU

3 **(a)** Look at diagram **A**. It tells you how to convert some metric units. On a copy, fill in the missing numbers. They are all 1, 10, 100 or 1000.

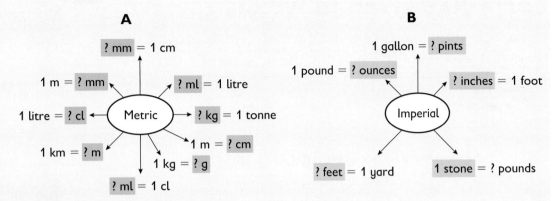

A

? mm = 1 cm

1 m = ? mm

? ml = 1 litre

1 litre = ? cl   Metric   ? kg = 1 tonne

1 km = ? m

1 m = ? cm

1 kg = ? g

? ml = 1 cl

B

1 gallon = ? pints

1 pound = ? ounces

? inches = 1 foot

Imperial

? feet = 1 yard

1 stone = ? pounds

(b) Now do the same for the imperial units in diagram **B**. You need the numbers 3, 8, 12, 14, 16.

4 Look at the bags of fruit in the picture. Match each question to the correct calculation.

(a) What is the weight of 4 bags of apples and 3 bags of pears?

A $2 \times 4 - 3 \times 3$

B $3 \times 3 - 2 \times 4$

(b) How much heavier are 3 bags of pears than 4 bags of apples?

C $3 \times 3 + 2 \times 4$

D $2 \times 4 + 3 \times 3$

APPLES 2 kg   PEARS 3 kg

5 **(a)** How many inches are there in
  (i) 2 ft   **(ii)** 5 ft   **(iii)** $1\frac{1}{2}$ ft?

(b) Change these lengths to feet.
  (i) 36 inches   **(ii)** 50 inches   **(iii)** 60 inches

6 The petrol tank in Mr Black's car holds 40 litres. Look at the petrol gauge.

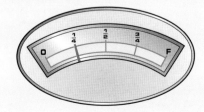

(a) How much petrol has Mr Black left in his tank?

(b) Mr Black fills up the tank. How much petrol does he put in?

Formulae given in words review

Christina plans to make a box for her design project.
She uses a formula to work out the volume of a box.

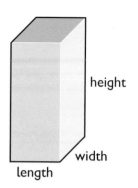

height

width

length

> Volume of box = length × width × height

Christina has designed three different boxes.

 What is the volume of each of these boxes?
What is a formula?

Box	length	width	height
1	6 m	4 cm	5 cm
2	5 cm	5 cm	5 cm
3	7 cm	3 cm	6 cm

Task

How much card do I need to make my box?

Christina

Christina can use this formula to help her:

> Area of a rectangle = length × width

1 How many faces does a box have?

2 What is the area of each face of Christina's box 1?

3 How much card does Christina need to make each box?

Christina puts ribbon round her box.
She works out the length of ribbon using the formula:

> Perimeter of a rectangle
> = 2 × length + 2 × width

Multiply first and then add your answers.

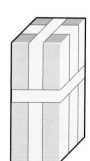

 What does 'perimeter' mean?

4 How much ribbon does Christina need for each box?

 Explain why Christina's formula for the perimeter works.

Exercise

1 Work out the area and perimeter of each of these rectangles.

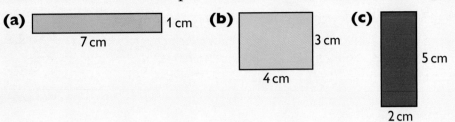

(a) 7 cm, 1 cm

(b) 4 cm, 3 cm

(c) 5 cm, 2 cm

2 Look at this sale advert.

SALE!!
Jeans   £30
Shirts   £20

(a) What is the cost of 2 pairs of jeans and 3 shirts? Show your working.

(b) (i) Copy and complete this formula.

Cost (£) = 30 × [   ] + [   ] × number of shirts

(ii) What is the cost of 4 pairs of jeans and 2 shirts?

3 You know someone's age in months.
This formula gives their age in years.

Age in years = age in months ÷ 12

Work out the ages of these people in years.

I'm 60 months

I'm 120 months

I'm 180 months

4 This is the formula to work out the area of a triangle.

Area = $\frac{1}{2}$ × base × height

Work out the area of these triangles.

(a) base = 4 cm and height = 6 cm

(b) base = 8 cm and height = 4 cm

(c) base = 3 cm and height = 8 cm

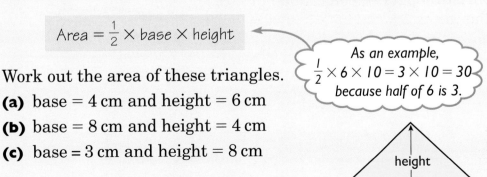

As an example,
$\frac{1}{2}$ × 6 × 10 = 3 × 10 = 30
because half of 6 is 3.

height

base

Formulae given in letters

Jo has £60 to spend.

I'm buying 4 CDs. How much change will I get?

CD Sale!!
Only £12 each!!

This is what Jo writes: Jo

Change (in pounds) = 60 – 12 × number of cds

? **Explain Jo's formula.**

Jo writes her formula using letters:

You don't need the × sign. So you can write C = 60 – 12n

$$C = 60 - 12 \times n$$
$$n = 4, \text{ so } \quad C = 60 - 12 \times 4$$

*C and n are **variables**. This means they stand for numbers which can change.*

? **What do C and n stand for?**
How much change does Jo get?

Task

1 Copy and complete this table:

Number of CDs	0	1	2	3	4	5
Change from £60						

2 Samir buys 2 CDs more than Jo.
So Samir buys $n + 2$ CDs.
How much does Samir spend when: **(a)** $n = 3$ **(b)** $n = 5$?

3 Match together these algebra cards.

2 more than n	$2 \times n$
2 plus n	$n + n$
$2n$	$n + 2$
2 less than n	$n \times 2$
n added to n	$n - 2$
twice n	$2 + n$

 How can you check you are right?

Exercise

1 Work out the value of $2 \times a + 3 \times b - 4 \times c$ when:

   (a) $a = 2$, $b = 3$ and $c = 1$
   (b) $a = 0$, $b = 3$ and $c = 2$
   (c) $a = 4$, $b = 0$ and $c = 2$
   (d) $a = 20$, $b = 30$ and $c = 5$

Remember BIDMAS

2 Work out the value of $5d + 2e - f$ when:

   (a) $d = 4$, $e = 3$ and $f = 2$
   (b) $d = 0$, $e = 1$ and $f = 2$
   (c) $d = 3$, $e = 7$ and $f = 1$
   (d) $d = 1$, $e = 2$ and $f = 6$

Remember, 5d means $5 \times d$

3 The formula to convert metres to centimetres is

$$c = 100m$$

where c stands for the number of centimetres and m stands for the number of metres.

Convert these measurements to centimetres.

   (a) 2 m   **(b)** 3 m   **(c)** 10 m

4 Ali uses a formula to work out the cost for her family.

$$cost = 16a + 8c$$

Avonford
Adventure Park
Adults £16   Children £8

   (a) What do a and c stand for?
   (b) How much does it cost for 2 adults and 3 children?
   (c) Ali pays £80.
        How many adults and children are there in Ali's family?
        Find as many answers as you can.

5 The formula for the area of a parallelogram is

$$area = b \times h$$

Work out the area of these parallelograms.

   (a) $b = 6$ cm and $h = 5$ cm
   (b) $b = 4$ cm and $h = 7$ cm

Finishing off

Now that you have finished this chapter you should:

- know the meanings of the words **formula** and **variable**
- be able to use a formula expressed in words
- be able to uses a formula expressed in letters
- be able to write down a formula using words and letters.

Review exercise

1 Work out the value of $4 \times a + 5 \times b - 2 \times c$ when

   (a) $a = 1$, $b = 2$ and $c = 0$ **(b)** $a = 3$, $b = 2$ and $c = 11$

   (c) $a = 4$, $b = 2$ and $c = 3$ **(d)** $a = 1$, $b = 1$ and $c = 1$.

2 Work out the value of $3a + b - 5c$ when

   (a) $a = 1$, $b = 3$ and $c = 0$ **(b)** $a = 4$, $b = 3$ and $c = 2$

   (c) $a = 4$, $b = 8$ and $c = 1$ **(d)** $a = 1$, $b = 1$ and $c = 0$.

3 Lucy wants to buy some music on the internet.
She looks at two websites.

(a) Copy and complete Lucy's formula for the cost of CDs.

> e-cds :   Cost (£) = _____ × number of cds + _____

(b) Write down a formula for the cost of CDs from Music.com.
(c) How much are 4 CDs from e-cds?
(d) How much are 5 CDs from Music.com?
(e) How much cheaper is it to buy 6 CDs from e-cds than from Music.com?

Lucy buys some CDs.
The cost at e-cds and Music.com is the same.

(f) How many CDs does she buy?

4 Look at these triangles.

  A

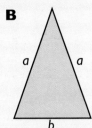 **B**

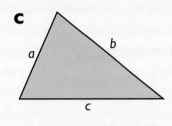 **C**

(a) Match together the triangles with the formulae for their perimeters.

(i) Perimeter = $a + b + c$

(ii) Perimeter = $2a + b$

(iii) Perimeter = $a + a + b$

(iv) Perimeter = $3a$

(v) Perimeter = $a + a + a$

(v) Perimeter = $c + b + a$

(b) Work out the perimeter of each triangle when
  (i) $a = 4$, $b = 2$ and $c = 3$
  (ii) $a = 5$, $b = 3$ and $c = 6$.

(c) (i) Is $3a$ always the same as $a + a + a$?
  (ii) Is $2a + b$ always the same as $a + a + b$?

5 The surface area of a cuboid is

surface area = $2lw + 2lh + 2wh$

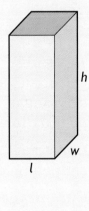

(a) Work out the surface area of these cuboids.

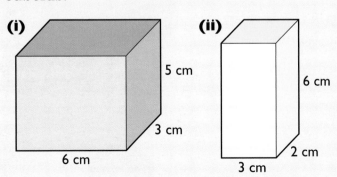

(i)   6 cm, 5 cm, 3 cm

(ii)   3 cm, 6 cm, 2 cm

(b) Explain how the formula works.

Shape review

Look at these shapes.

Some are flat and some are solid.

? **What are the names of the shapes?**

? **Which of them are 2-D shapes?**
Which are 3-D?

? **What does 3-D mean?**

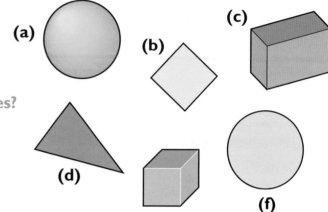

(a) (b) (c) (d) (e) (f)

Task

Humza is making a child's toy for his Design and Technology project.

The toy is a posting tower in the shape of a cuboid.

Humza has made these 3-D shapes for the project. Each shape will fit through only **one** hole in the posting tower.

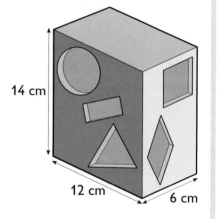

14 cm

12 cm   6 cm

The holes must be cut out accurately.

1 Construct a suitable scale drawing of a net for Humza's posting tower.

2 Construct to scale the correct shaped holes in the net.

3 Cut out the net and the holes, and fold the net to make a model of the posting tower.

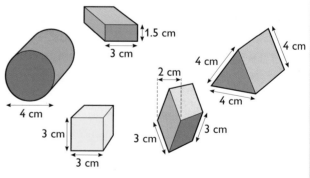

1.5 cm
3 cm
4 cm
4 cm
4 cm
2 cm
3 cm
4 cm
3 cm
3 cm
3 cm

? **What shape is Humza describing?**

I've made a 3-D shape with six rectangular faces, twelve edges and eight vertices.

Humza

Exercise

1 Fill in a copy of the table by sorting these shapes into 2-D and 3-D shapes.

cylinder square sphere

cuboid hexagon pyramid

cube triangle circle

rectangle

2-D shapes	3-D shapes

2

This is a 2-D shape with three sides and three angles. The sides are 9 cm, 8 cm and 7 cm long.

Samir

Construct an accurate drawing of Samir's shape.

3

This is a 3-D shape with one curved face and two flat, circular faces.

What shape is Jo describing?   Jo

Activity Some 3-D shapes can be drawn on **isometric** paper.

Practise using isometric paper to draw different cubes and cuboids.

Then draw your initials on isometric paper.

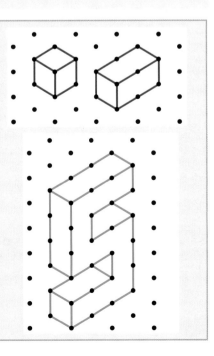

Triangles and quadrilaterals

Some of these shapes are triangles and some are quadrilaterals.

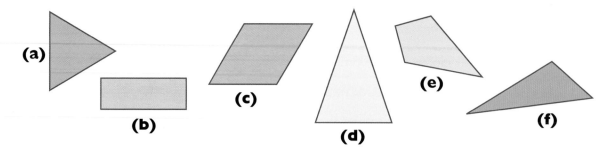

(a) **(b)** **(c)** **(d)** **(e)** **(f)**

 What is the difference between a triangle and a quadrilateral?

 What are the special names for each of the shapes?

Task

Sophie has used a 3 by 3 grid on square dotted paper to draw this triangle.

 What sort of triangle is it?

I can make 8 different triangles in a 3 by 3 grid.

Sophie

 What does Sophie mean by 'different'?

On square dotted paper, draw and name all 8 triangles.

 Is it possible to draw an equilateral triangle on a 3 by 3 grid?

Ali describes a square.

 What does parallel mean?

 Describe a rectangle.

 Describe a kite.

A square is a quadrilateral with four right angles and four equal sides. The opposite sides of a square are parallel.

Ali

Exercise

1

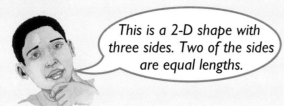

Karl

This is a 2-D shape with three sides. Two of the sides are equal lengths.

(a) Sketch the shape that Karl is describing.
(b) What is the name of the shape?

2 (a) How many lines of symmetry does an equilateral triangle have?

(b) How many lines of symmetry does a kite have?

3 Christina has drawn this quadrilateral.

(a) What is the special name for the quadrilateral?

(b) How many more quadrilaterals can you draw on a 3 by 3 grid?
Draw and name each one.

Activity Construct these shapes accurately.

(a)

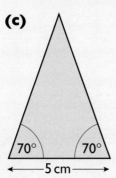

5 cm   5 cm

5 cm

(b)

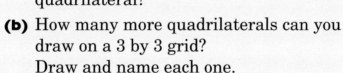

6 cm

4.5 cm   4.5 cm

45°   135°

6 cm

(c)

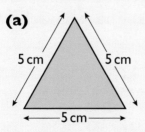

70°   70°

5 cm

(d)

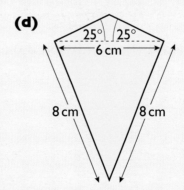

25° 25°
6 cm

8 cm   8 cm

What is the name of each shape?

Nets

This box holds sandwiches.

 What shape are the side faces of the box?
What shape are the other faces?

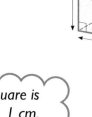

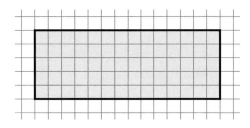

14 cm

14 cm   5 cm

Sam draws the net for the box.
He starts by drawing this face.

*Each square is
1 cm × 1 cm.*

 Which face has Sam drawn?

Task

I   On squared paper, complete the net for the sandwich box.
Remember to add flaps.

2   Decorate the box to show what sandwiches are inside.

3   Cut the net out and glue it together to make the sandwich box.

Look at the sandwich box you have made.

 How many faces, edges and vertices does it have?

In the supermarket, the sandwich boxes
are displayed like this.

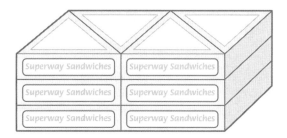

Superway Sandwiches   Superway Sandwiches
Superway Sandwiches   Superway Sandwiches
Superway Sandwiches   Superway Sandwiches

 In what other ways can you display all the boxes made by the class?

Exercise

1 This is the net of a cuboid.

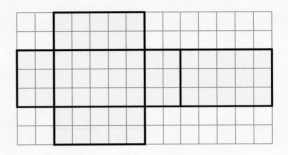

Each square is 1 cm by 1 cm.

(a) How long is the cuboid?
(b) How wide is the cuboid?
(c) How high is the cuboid?
(d) Work out the volume of the cuboid.

2 These are the nets of two cuboids.

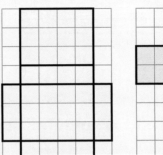

(a) Do the cuboids have the same volume?
How do you know?

(b) Do the cuboids have the same surface area?
How do you know?

3 Draw the net for this shape.

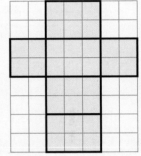

2 cm

5 cm

12 cm

Activity Some of these drawings are nets of cubes and some are not.

Copy the drawings, cut them out and test them.

Which drawings are the nets of cubes?

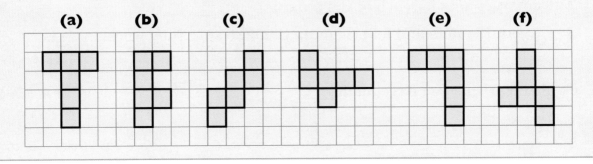

(a) **(b)** **(c)** **(d)** **(e)** **(f)**

Prisms

Look at this packet of chocolate.

? How many faces does it have?
How many edges?
How many vertices?

? What shape is each face?

The shape is called a **triangular prism**.
The cross-section of a prism is the same all along its length.

Task

1 Which of these shapes are **prisms**?

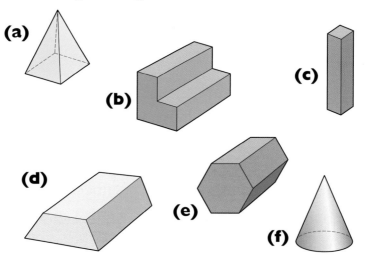

(a)
(b)
(c)
(d)
(e)
(f)

2 Construct nets for each of the **prisms**.

3 Cut out the nets and fold them up to make sure they work.

Look at the prisms you have made.

 How many faces, edges and vertices does the L-shaped
prism have?

Exercise

1 **(a)** What is the name of each of these shapes?

(i) **(ii)**

(b) Is each shape a prism?

(c) How many faces, edges and vertices does each shape have?

2 This is a net for a prism.

(a) What shape are the end faces of the prism?

(b) How many faces, edges and vertices does the prism have?

3 Look at this cuboid.

(a) What is its volume?

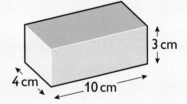

The cuboid is cut along its diagonal.

(b) What is the name of the two new shapes?

(c) What is the volume of one of the new shapes?

(d) Write down a formula for finding the volume of a triangular prism.

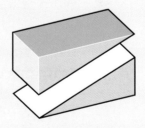

Remember:
Volume of a cuboid is
length × width × height.

Activity Design a small gift box that is a prism.

Draw the net for your box on thin card, decorate it, cut it out and glue it together.

Finishing off

Now that you have finished this chapter you should be able to:

- recognise and describe common 2-D and 3-D shapes
- recognise equilateral, isosceles and scalene triangles
- recognise and describe common quadrilaterals
- recognise nets for cubes, cuboids, prisms and other solids
- draw nets of cubes, cuboids, prisms and other solids.

Review exercise

1 Look at these nets of shapes.

(a)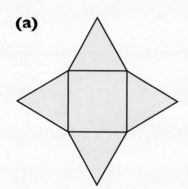

(b)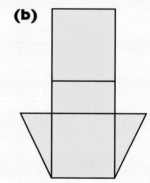

What shape does each net make?

2 Use a ruler, compasses and protractor to construct accurate drawings of these shapes.

(a) A rhombus

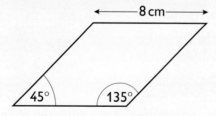

(b) A regular 9-sided polygon

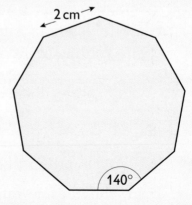

su

3 Find the shape words in this wordsearch.

There are 17 words to find. Can you find them all?

These pictures will help you.

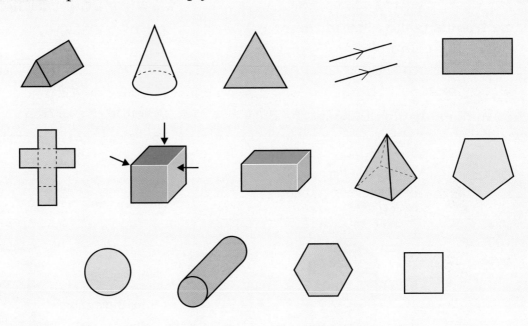

R	V	B	Y	E	N	L	W	F	Z	N	F
D	E	D	G	E	C	E	N	C	O	N	C
P	R	C	P	P	Y	C	T	G	B	O	M
V	T	U	T	R	L	R	A	H	N	G	P
T	E	B	I	A	I	T	I	E	D	A	R
U	X	E	L	A	N	S	F	I	R	X	P
X	Y	C	N	E	D	G	M	A	E	E	B
J	A	G	P	I	E	A	L	L	C	H	K
P	L	N	O	X	R	L	C	E	V	E	K
E	T	B	P	Y	E	R	A	U	Q	S	Y
R	U	I	P	L	I	Q	G	W	U	S	E
C	P	T	B	C	U	X	D	P	C	Q	I

4 Data display

Data display review

Some friends make a list of their favourite TV channels.

BBC 1	Channel 4	ITV 1
BBC 2	ITV 1	BBC 1
ITV 1	ITV 1	BBC 1
ITV 1	ITV 1	ITV 1
Channel 5	Channel 5	ITV 1
BBC 1	BBC 1	BBC 1
Channel 5	Channel 4	BBC 2
ITV 1	Channel 4	BBC 2

They make a display to show the data.

We must find the frequency for each channel.

Megan

We could draw a bar chart …

Harry

… or a pie chart.

Michelle

? How many items of data are there?

? Make a tally chart for these data.

? Which is the most popular channel?

Task

1 Draw a bar chart to show these data.

2 Draw a pictogram to show these data.

You will need to choose a symbol to represent 1 person's choice.

3 What fraction chose BBC 1?

4 Why do you use an angle of 90° to show this on a pie chart?

5 Work out the angles for BBC 2, ITV 1, Channel 4 and Channel 5.

6 Draw a pie chart.

7 Make a class poster with your data displays.

? Look at your displays.
Which display shows the data best?

Exercise

1 Humza asks his friends to name their favourite football team. Here are the results.

Team	Frequency
Manchester United	10
Liverpool	12
Arsenal	16
Aston Villa	6
Leeds United	8

Draw a bar chart and a pictogram to display these data.

2 Andy has drawn this pie chart to show the nationalities of his pen friends.

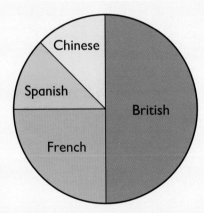

(a) What nationality are half of Andy's pen friends?

(b) What fraction of Andy's pen friends are French?

(c) Andy has 16 pen friends. How many are
   (i) British   **(ii)** French
   (iii) Spanish   **(iv)** Chinese?

Activity   Ask 8 people to name a fruit.

Make a tally chart of the results.

Display the results on a pie chart.

Instead, this could be an animal, a football team, a country or any idea of your own.

2-way tables

There is a traffic problem outside Avonford School. Too many students travel by car.

There is a school bus for anyone more than 3 miles away.

This is a 2-way table.

The council do a survey of how students get to school.

Distance from school	Means of transport					
	Walk	**Cycle**	**Car**	**Bus**	**Train**	**Total**
Less than 3 miles	10	111	161	15	2	
3 miles or more	0	15	59	34	70	
Total						

? Why is this called a 2-way table?

? How many students live less than 3 miles from school and come to school by car?

? Copy the table and fill in the totals.

? How many students walk to school?

Task

Below is a 2-way table.
Find out how the students in your class come to school.
Copy and complete this 2-way table.

	Means of transport					
	Walk	**Cycle**	**Car**	**Bus**	**Train**	**Total**
Boys						
Girls						
Total						

? How do the totals help you to check your table?

Exercise

1 This 2-way table shows the sales of drinks in Annie's café.

Day	Tea	Coffee	Squash	Milk	Total
Monday	5	12	10	4	
Tuesday	11	15	7	2	
Wednesday	10	19	6	5	
Thursday	9	12	35	3	
Friday	23	47	10	4	
Saturday	12	21	11	2	
Total					

(The column group spanning Tea, Coffee, Squash, Milk is headed **Drink**.)

(a) How many cups of coffee did Annie sell on Wednesday?

(b) Copy the table and fill in the totals.

(c) A class of school students came to the café one day in the week. Which day was this?

(d) A group of pensioners meets at the café one day each week. Which day do they meet?

2 This 2-way table shows the types of houses in 3 streets in Avonford. Some numbers are missing.

Street	Bungalow	Terraced	Semi-Detached	Detached	Total
Ascot Drive	10	6	12		40
Mill Lane		12	22		52
London Road					
Total	25	32	46	34	

(The column group spanning Bungalow, Terraced, Semi-Detached, Detached is headed **Type of house**.)

(a) There are 9 bungalows in Mill Lane. Show this in a copy of the table.

(b) How many detached houses are in Ascot Drive?

(c) How many detached houses are in Mill Lane?

(d) On your copy, fill in the numbers of each type of house in London Road.

Stem-and-leaf diagrams

Pete draws a stem-and-leaf diagram on his computer to show the heights of students in his class.

Pete

I am 165 cm tall.

The heights of students in 9G

Stem	Leaf
15	0 3 5 5 6 6 7 7 8
16	0 0 1 1 3 3 3 4 5 5 5 6 7 7
17	1 2 3 5 6 7 7

Key   16 | 5 means 165 cm

? Find Pete's height in the diagram.

? How tall is Jack? Are you sure?

2 other people are the same height as me.

Jack

Task

Measure the heights of everyone in your class.
Write a list of the heights. Rewrite the list with the heights in order.
Use a grid like this to draw a stem-and-leaf diagram.

Stem	Leaf
15	
16	

Give your diagram a title. Write a key for your diagram.

? Which is better, a tally chart or a stem-and-leaf diagram?

I think it looks like a tally chart.

Pete

Exercise

1 Jo's class are asked to guess the length of a line.
Their guesses are displayed in this stem-and-leaf diagram.

Stem	Leaf
3	1 1 5 8
4	2 4 6 ⑥ 7 9 9
5	0 2 4 5 7 8 8 8 9
6	3 4 5 7 7 8
7	0 1 4 5 5

Key 5/4 means 54 cm

(a) What number is represented by the entry circled in red?

(b) Write down the highest guess and the lowest guess.

(c) How many students are in the class?

You need to find the middle number.

(d) Find the median guess.

(e) What is the mode of the guesses?

This is the most common guess.

2 Here are the times in minutes that members of Avonford Athletics Club took to run a marathon.

150, 151, 151, 166, 173, 189, 191, 193, 197, 203, 214, 219, 220, 223, 227, 231, 234, 236, 237, 239

(a) Display these times in a stem-and-leaf diagram.
Copy the diagram which has been started for you.

Stem	Leaf
15	0 1 1
16	6

(b) Give your diagram a title.

(c) Add a key to your diagram.

Finishing off

Now that you have finished this chapter you should be able to:
• draw and interpret bar charts and pie charts
• read 2-way tables
• draw-stem-and leaf diagrams.

Review exercise

1 This 2-way table is an order form for the sandwiches for the office staff in a large company.

Office	Type of sandwich			
	Cheese	**Ham**	**Prawn**	**Salad**
Manager	3	2	1	3
Accounts	7	3	5	4
Secretaries	1	2	6	9
Maintenance	21	19	3	5

(a) Work out the totals for each row and column.

(b) How many cheese sandwiches are ordered?

(c) How many sandwiches are ordered for the manager's office?

2 Lucy has drawn a stem-and-leaf diagram to show the attendance at her local football club's matches last season.

10	2 4 7
11	6 7 8 8 8 9
12	0 1 3 5
13	6
14	2 3 5 8
15	9

Key 13 | 6 means 136

(a) 120 people attended one match.
How is this shown in the diagram?

(b) Write down the lowest attendance.

(c) Write down the highest attendance.

(d) What is the range for these data?

(e) How many matches did the team play?

3 Mercy has a newspaper round.
This bar chart shows how many papers she delivers each day in one week.

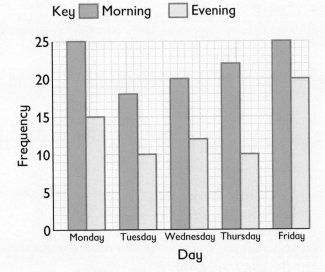

(a) How many papers does she deliver on Monday evening?
(b) How many papers does she deliver on Wednesday?
(c) How many morning papers does she deliver in the week?
(d) Mercy delivers more morning papers than evening papers.
How many more?

Activity Collect some data of your own.

I want to know people's favourite football team.

Alan

I am going to ask 10 boys and 10 girls to choose their favourite subject.

Can I measure everybody's hand span?

Meena

Mark

Choose an appropriate way to display your data.

Make a class poster to show your displays.

Make sure that you have at least one example of each type of display.

I am going to use a stem and leaf diagram.

John

I want to draw a 2-way table. What sort of information should I collect?

Kim

Cross number

Ask your teacher for a copy of the puzzle opposite.
Answer these clues to fill it in.

Across

2 Look at this formula.

> length in inches = length in feet × 12

A piece of wood is 2 feet long.
How many inches long is it?

3 127×1000

5 The number of degrees in a whole turn.

6 9237 rounded to the nearest 1000

7 These are heights of sunflower plants in centimetres.

18	2 7
19	0 3 4
20	1 1 3 5 9
21	0 0 ⑥ 7
22	2 7

Key **18** | 7 = 187 cm

What height is represented by the entry circled in red?

10 The pie chart shows the favourite sport of 420 students.
How many students prefer cricket?

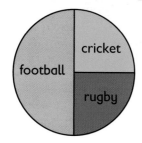

11 20 minutes after 1834 hours

14 25 multiplied by 5

15 3280×100

16 8^2

Down

1 The number of centimetres in a metre.

2 Twenty thousand, four hundred and ninety-six, written in numbers.

4 The perimeter of this rectangle, calculated in metres.

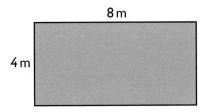

5 35×1000

8 $20\,000 - 3175$

9 147×100, then add 34

12 The angles in a triangle add up to ▢ degrees.

13 $\frac{1}{2} = $ ▢ %

Ratio review

Pete and Jack are designing a new football shirt for their school. The school colours are purple and yellow.

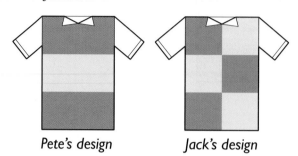

Pete's design   Jack's design

Pete's design is 1 part yellow and 2 parts purple.   yellow : purple = 1 : 2

? **What is the ratio of the colours for Jack's design?**

? **Write the ratio in its simplest form.**

A ratio in its simplest form uses the smallest possible numbers.

Task

1 Look at these designs by other students. Write down the ratios of yellow : purple. Write each answer in the simplest form.

(a)   **(b)**   **(c)**   **(d)**   **(e)**   **(f)**

    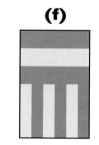

2 Design your own football shirt using the ratio, yellow : purple = 2 : 3.

All the school doors are purple. The purple paint is made by mixing red and blue paint in the ratio 1 : 2.

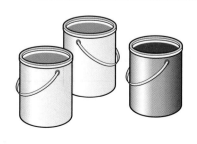

? **What does this ratio mean?**

Karl mixes 2 litres of red with 6 litres of blue paint.

? **Does he make the correct purple colour?**

Exercise

1 Write down the ratio for each picture in its simplest form.

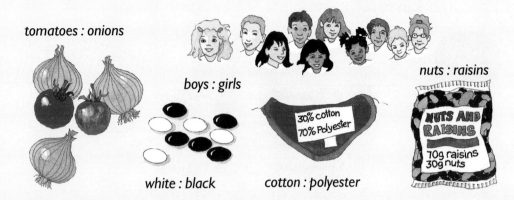

tomatoes : onions

boys : girls

30% cotton
70% Polyester

nuts : raisins

NUTS AND RAISINS

70g raisins
30g nuts

white : black

cotton : polyester

2 Which of these ratios are the same as 1 : 2?

2 : 4   6 : 8   6 : 10   6 : 12   3 : 6

3 To make a 'Saint Clement' drink, you use
4 cl of lemonade and 6 cl of orange.
Write down the ratio of lemonade to
orange in its simplest form.

SU

4 On a copy, match the ratios. The first one has been done for you.

2 : 3   30 : 40

3 : 4   5 : 20

4 : 7   8 : 14

5 : 7   6 : 9

1 : 4   8 : 20

2 : 5   25 : 35

Activity Throw 2 dice, one red, the other green.
Write down the 2 numbers as a ratio,
red : green.
Cancel this ratio if you can.
What are the possible answers?

2 : 4 = 1 : 2

Sharing

Humza and Lucy buy a chocolate bar between them.

Humza

I will split it in half.

That's not fair! I paid 45p and you only paid 15p.

Lucy

They decide to split the chocolate in the ratio 1 : 3.

 Why do they decide on 1 : 3?

There are 12 pieces of chocolate.

 How many pieces do they each get?

Humza and Lucy share more of the same type of chocolate bars.
Copy and complete the table. You have already done the first one above.

Money paid		Ratio	Pieces of chocolate	
Humza	Lucy		Humza	Lucy
15p	45p	1 : 3		
10p	50p			
20p	40p			
5p	55p			
25p	35p			
30p	30p			

Two neighbours club together to buy some lottery tickets.
Mrs Patel puts in £6 and Mrs Jones puts in £4.
One of their tickets wins £50 000.

 In what ratio should they share the prize money?

 How much do they each win?

Exercise

SU

1 Colour in a copy of these sticks in the following ratios.

(a) [stick diagram]   1:4 red:white

(b) [stick diagram]   2:3 blue:white

(c) [stick diagram]   1:5 yellow:white

(d) [stick diagram]   1:2 black:white

(e) [stick diagram]   1:1 green:yellow

(f) [stick diagram]   3:5 green:white

2 Orange squash is made up of 1 part squash to 5 parts water.

(a) Write this as a ratio.
(b) How much water do you add to 10 ml of squash?
(c) How much orange juice do you get?

3 Orange paint is made up of red and yellow paint in the ratio, red:yellow = 2:3.

Alan wants to make 10 litres of orange paint.
How much of each colour does he need?

4 A school trip is made up of teachers and students in the ratio 1:10. There are 100 students on the trip. How many teachers are there?

Activity A stick is 10 cm long.
The stick is cut into 2 lengths. Here is an example:

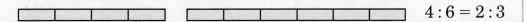   4:6 = 2:3

How many other ways can you split the stick?

For each way, write down the ratio in its simplest form.

Similar figures

Class 9G are making bird boxes for their design project. Meena draws the front of hers on the computer. She then tries to enlarge her drawing in the ratio 1 : 2.

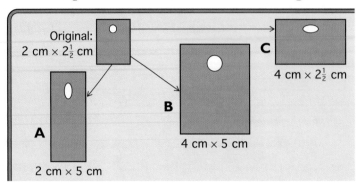

Original:
2 cm × 2½ cm

C

4 cm × 2½ cm

B

4 cm × 5 cm

A

2 cm × 5 cm

A ratio of 1 : 2 for an enlargement is called a scale factor of 2.

  Which drawing is a correct enlargement?
What has she done wrong with the others?

Task

Harry's drawing of the front of his box measures 2 cm by 3 cm. He uses this diagram to work out possible measurements for the actual box.

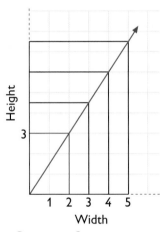

Height

3

1 2 3 4 5
Width

New width	New height	Scale factor
3 cm	4.5 cm	1.5
4 cm	6 cm	
5 cm		2.5
6 cm		
7 cm		
8 cm		

I On graph paper, copy and complete Harry's diagram.
The width increases by 1 cm for each rectangle up to 8 cm wide.

2 Copy and complete his table.

  A shape and its enlargement are similar.
Who is right, Mark or Christina?

Similar means same shape but maybe different size.

No, similar means same size but maybe different shape.

Mark

Christina

Exercise

1 Enlarge this shape.
Use a ratio of 1 : 3.

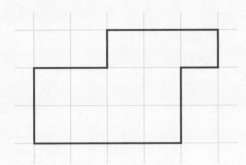

2 This shape has been enlarged using a ratio of 1 : 2.
Draw the original shape.

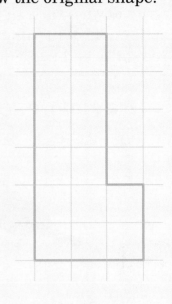

3 Look at this rectangle.

2 cm

◄1 cm►

Which of the following rectangles are similar?

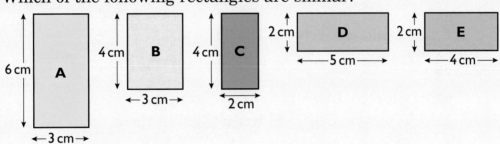

6 cm **A**

◄3 cm►

4 cm **B**

◄3 cm►

4 cm **C**

2 cm

2 cm **D**

◄5 cm►

2 cm **E**

◄4 cm►

4 These triangles are similar.
What is their ratio?

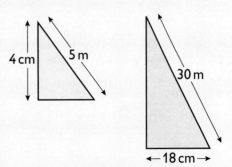

4 cm   5 m

30 m

◄18 cm►

5 Look at this bridge.

How many pairs of similar triangles can you see?

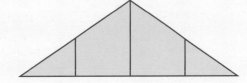

Finishing off

Now that you have finished this chapter you should be able to:

- write down a ratio in its simplest form
- split an amount into two parts
- recognise and use similar figures.

Review exercise

1 At 10 am, Tim records the birds he sees in the garden.

(a) Write down the ratio, blackbirds : sparrows.

At 11 am, Tim does the same thing again. This time, there are 2 blackbirds and 8 sparrows.

(b) Write down the ratio, blackbirds : sparrows in the simplest form.

At midday the ratio is 1 : 3.

(c) There are 4 blackbirds. How many sparrows are there?

2 Which of these ratios can be cancelled down?
Copy them out and write them in their simplest form.

| 1 : 3 | 2 : 4 | 4 : 2 | 3 : 9 | 2 : 5 | 5 : 20 |

3 In a competition, Class 9G wins a prize of £50 to spend on their classroom. They decide to buy some new posters. However, the girls and boys cannot decide what posters to buy.

I know, Miss. Give the boys £25 and the girls £25. Then we can decide separately.

Kim

That is not fair, Miss. There are 15 boys in the class and only 10 girls. The boys should get more money to spend.

Jack

Use Jack's suggestion.

(a) How much money do the boys get?
Show how you work this out.

(b) How much money do the girls get?
Show how you work this out.

4 In the Canary Islands you can buy bottles filled with different coloured sands.
This one only has 2 different colours in the ratio,
red : white = 1 : 4.

Colour in a copy of the bottle.

5 **(a)** Use squared paper.
Enlarge the picture of this cuboid.
Use a scale factor of 3.

(b) What word is used to describe the 2 cuboids?

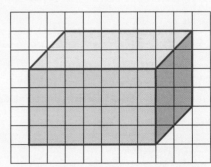

Activity On squared paper, copy and continue this pattern.
It produces 2 sets of similar shapes.

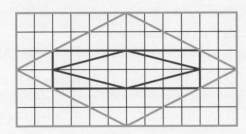

Balancing equations

Look at Lucy's see-saw.
It is balanced.
Karl works out Lucy's weight.

$L + 20 = 70$
Take 20 from both sides $\quad L + 20 - 20 = 70 - 20$
$\underline{L = 50}$

> The equation **balances** because the 20 was subtracted from both sides.

? **What does ℓ stand for?**

Karl has **solved** the equation.

? **Karl has done the same thing to both sides of the equation. Explain why.**

? **Explain how you would solve these equations.**

(a) $a - 20 = 70$ **(b)** $b \times 3 = 12$ **(c)** $\dfrac{c}{4} = 5$

Task

1 Find the missing whole number values.
How many different answers can you find?

(a) ☐ + ▲ = 4 **(b)** ☐ × ▲ = 12

2 Solve these equations.
Match your answers to the letters to crack the code.

(a) $x + 7 = 12$ **(b)** $x - 4 = 5$ **(c)** $x \times 5 = 20$

(d) $\dfrac{x}{3} = 4$ **(e)** $x \times 3 = 27$ **(f)** $x - 2 = 1$

(g) $x - 7 = 5$ **(h)** $x + 3 = 10$ **(i)** $7 + x = 8$

A	$x = 9$
C	$x = 1$
D	$x = 2$
F	$x = 5$
I	$x = 7$
L	$x = 8$
N	$x = 4$
P	$x = 6$
S	$x = 3$
T	$x = 12$

? **Look at Karl's working.**

$3a = 21$
÷ both sides by 3 $\quad 3a \div 3 = 21 \div 3$
$\underline{a = 7}$

What does 3a mean?
Explain Karl's working.

> You write 3a not a3.
> Numbers first, then letters.

Exercise

1 How much do these children weigh?

(a)

(b)

2 Solve these equations.
    (a) $a + 7 = 12$ **(b)** $b + 13 = 28$ **(c)** $c - 4 = 1$
    (d) $d - 12 = 7$ **(e)** $e + 9 = 10$ **(f)** $f - 9 = 3$

3 Solve these equations.
    (a) $a \times 4 = 16$ **(b)** $b \times 13 = 26$ **(c)** $9e = 36$
    (d) $d \div 2 = 15$ **(e)** $\dfrac{c}{4} = 2$ **(f)** $\dfrac{f}{5} = 4$

4 Solve these equations.
    (a) $a + 3 = 8$ **(b)** $b - 7 = 1$ **(c)** $1 + c = 14$
    (d) $\dfrac{d}{12} = 2$ **(e)** $2e = 10$ **(f)** $7 + f = 18$
    (g) $4g = 32$ **(h)** $\dfrac{h}{9} = 1$ **(i)** $4 + i = 17$

5 Look at these scales. They are balanced.
Find the weight of each parcel.

The parcels on each set of scales are the same.

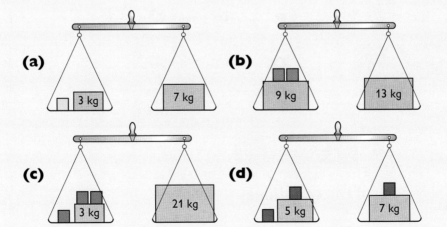

Solving equations

Mark is solving this equation.

$$3a + 6 = 18$$

Look at Mark's working.

Take 6 from both sides
$$3a + 6 = 18$$
$$3a + 6 - 6 = 18 - 6$$
Tidy up
$$3a = 12$$

Does Mark's equation balance?
What is the value of *a*?

Explain how you would solve these equations.

(a) $5n + 3 = 13$ (b) $6c - 7 = 11$

Task

Sophie and Mark are playing **Equation match-up**.
They each write down 4 numbers between 1 and 10.

| 3   5   4   10 |

Sophie's numbers

| 1   2   3   9 |

Mark's numbers

They take a card from the pack and solve the equation on it.
When the answer matches one of their numbers they cross it out.
The winner is the first person to cross out all 4 numbers.

Here are the cards from the pack.

A $3a + 6 = 18$ **B** $2n - 1 = 11$

C $4a + 2 = 10$ **D** $2m - 1 = 1$

E $c - 6 = 4$ **F** $5b + 2 = 17$

G $3e - 12 = 15$

1 (a) Solve each of the equations.
  (b) Who wins?

2 Play your own game of **Equation match-up** with a partner.

How can you check your answers?

Exercise

1 Solve these equations.

(a) $2a + 1 = 5$ (b) $3b + 6 = 27$

(c) $5c - 4 = 16$ (d) $3 + 7d = 10$

(e) $3 + 6e = 15$ (f) $6f - 5 = 1$

(g) $10g - 22 = 38$ (h) $3h - 6 = 0$

2 Ali writes down a formula to work out the cost of a meal for her family.

> *Any*
> *3-course meal*
> *£12 per person*
> *plus*
> *£5 service charge per table*

$$\text{Cost} = 12_p + 5$$

(a) What does p stand for?

(b) How much is a meal for 6 people?

(c) The bill is £53.
How many people are there in Ali's family?

3 Meena and Alan are having an argument.

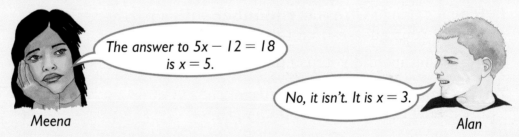

The answer to $5x - 12 = 18$ is $x = 5$.

No, it isn't. It is $x = 3$.

Meena   Alan

(a) Who is right?

(b) How can you tell an answer is wrong?

(c) What is the right answer?

4 This is the formula for the area of a rectangle.

$$\text{area} = \text{length} \times \text{width}$$

Find the length of each of these rectangles.

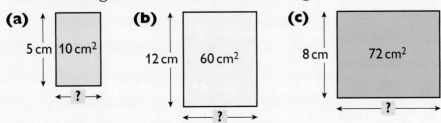

(a) 5 cm 10 cm² ?

(b) 12 cm 60 cm² ?

(c) 8 cm 72 cm² ?

Checking answers – trial and improvement

Pete and Mercy are playing **Guess my number**.

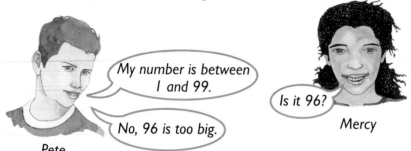

My number is between 1 and 99.

Is it 96?

No, 96 is too big.

Mercy

Pete

Mercy makes a table of her guesses.

   Why does Mercy write 0 and 100 first?
Her first guess is 96. What is her second guess?
What is her third guess?
What would be a sensible next guess? Why?

Too small	Too big
0	100
0	96
18	96
60	96

Task

1 Play a game of **Guess my number** with a partner.
Record your guesses in a table like Mercy did.

What method did you use to choose your next guess?

2 This square has an area of 70 cm².
Look how Pete works out its length.

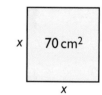

x | 70 cm²

x

Try $x = 10$ $10 \times 10 = 100$ too big
Try $x = 5$ $5 \times 5 = 25$ too small

This method is called trial and improvement.

So x is between 5 and 10.

(a) What is a sensible number to try next?
(b) Which two whole numbers is x between?
(c) Which number should you try next?
(d) Continue trying numbers.
Work out the length of the square as accurately as you can.

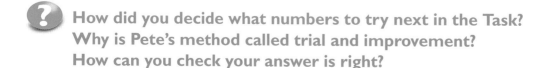

How did you decide what numbers to try next in the Task?
Why is Pete's method called trial and improvement?
How can you check your answer is right?

Exercise

1 Megan and Harry are playing a game of **Guess my number**.

(a) What should Megan's first guess be?

Harry says it is too small.

(b) What should Megan guess next?

My number is between 1 and 9.

Harry

2

The square root of 13 is between 3 and 4. I know, because $3^2 = 9$ and $4^2 = 16$.

$3^2 = 3 \times 3 = 9$ So the square root of 9 is 3.

Megan

Which whole numbers does the square root of each of these numbers lie between?

(a) 19 **(b)** 55 **(c)** 90 **(d)** 130

3 John and Michelle are working out the length of this square.

x | 40 cm²

x

It is 6.3 cm to one decimal place.

No, it is 6.4 cm.

John

Michelle

(a) Calculate these. **(i)** 6.3×6.3 **(ii)** 6.4×6.4

(b) (i) What is the difference between your answers to **(a)(i)** and **(ii)** and 40?

(ii) Who is right? Why?

4 Work out the length of these squares.
Give your answers to one decimal place.

(a) x 20 cm²
x

(b) x 60 cm²
x

(c) x 120 cm²
x

Finishing off

Now that you have finished this chapter you should be able to:

- know what an equation is
- solve an equation
- check your solution to an equation
- use trial and improvement to solve a problem.

Review exercise

1 Solve these equations.

(a) $a + 7 = 11$ (b) $b - 6 = 6$ (c) $3c = 33$

(d) $\dfrac{d}{6} = 2$ (e) $2e - 1 = 3$ (f) $4f + 3 = 7$

(g) $\dfrac{g}{4} = 5$ (h) $5h - 3 = 12$ (i) $\dfrac{i}{2} = 1$

2 Here is Jamie's maths homework:

> ### Maths Homework
>
> 1. $5x - 3 = 7$ Ans: $x = 2$ 2. $7x + 3 = 10$ Ans: $x = 3$
> 3. $9x - 4 = 14$ Ans: $x = 2$ 4. $5 - 3x = 2$ Ans: $x = 1$
> 5. $4 + 2x = 10$ Ans: $x = 4$ 6. $3x - 1 = 26$ Ans: $x = 8$

(a) Check Jamie's homework **without** solving the equations.

(b) Jamie got some questions wrong. Find the correct answers.

3 Jo has a pencils and Humza has b pencils.
Write in words the meaning of each equation below.

(a) $a = 8$ (b) $a + b = 12$ (c) $a = 2b$

4 Work out the length of these squares. Use trial and improvement.
Give your answers to one decimal place.

(a)

x | $30\,\text{cm}^2$
x

(b)

x | $95\,\text{cm}^2$
x

(c)

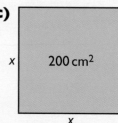

x | $200\,\text{cm}^2$
x

5 Ali and Tim are playing the **Guess my number** game.

I think of a number and multiply it by 2. Then I add 6. The answer is 14.

Ali

I think of a number and multiply it by 3. Then I add 7. The answer is 40.

Tim

Tim writes down the equation for Ali's mystery number.

$2n + 6 = 14$

(a) What does n stand for?

(b) Solve the equation to find Ali's mystery number.

(c) Write down an equation for Tim's mystery number.

(d) What is Tim's mystery number?

Activity

Kim is making a chicken run against a long wall.
She has 32 m of fencing.

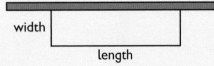

width

length

Kim wants to make the largest possible area.
Kim writes this question.

$l + 2w = 32$

1 What do ℓ and w stand for?

Kim tries different lengths for her chicken run.

When $l = 2$
$2 + 2w = 32$

2 When the length is 2 m, what is the width?
What is the area of the chicken run?

3 Copy and complete Kim's table.

Length, l	Equation	Width, w	Area = $l \times w$
2	$2 + 2w = 32$		
4	$4 + 2w = 32$	14	56
6			
8			

4 What is the largest possible area for the chickens?

Angles review

? Look at these angles.
How do you describe them?

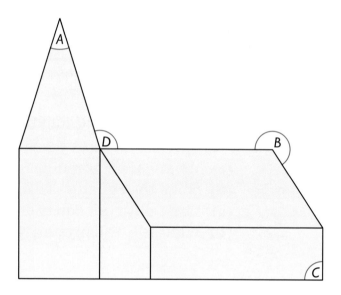

? How are angles measured?

? Measure the sizes of the angles in the diagram.

Task

1 Use only a ruler to draw angles as close as you can to these sizes.
   (a) 90° **(b)** 30° **(c)** 60° **(d)** 45° **(e)** 210°

2 Now use your protractor to measure your angles.
   How close are they?

? What do angles on
a straight line add
up to?

? What about angles
in a full turn?

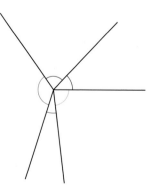

Exercise

1 Use a ruler and protractor to draw these angles accurately:
   (a) 80°   **(b)** 110°   **(c)** 40°   **(d)** 25°   **(e)** 166°

2 Look at this compass.

   (a) What are the compass directions of lines **(i)**, **(ii)** and **(iii)**?
   (b) Work out the angles that directions **(i)**, **(ii)** and **(iii)** make with the north line (going clockwise from north).

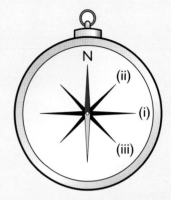

3 Work out the size of the missing angle in each of these diagrams.

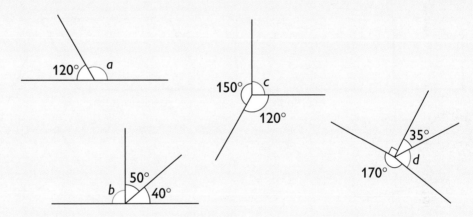

Activity

Play **Guess the angle** with a friend.

Using just a ruler, draw any angle.
Ask a friend to guess the size of the angle.
Measure the angle with a protractor.

If the guess is within 5° of the real size, your friend scores a point, if not, you score a point.

Take turns to draw and guess.

Angles in triangles and quadrilaterals

? What do the three angles of
a triangle add up to?

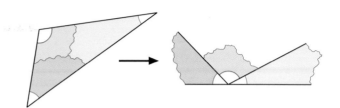

? How do you know?

Task

I Use a ruler to draw one of each of these sorts of quadrilaterals.

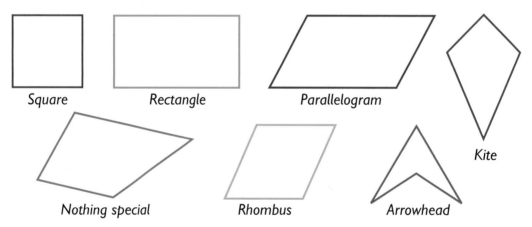

Square   Rectangle   Parallelogram

Nothing special   Rhombus   Arrowhead   Kite

2 For each of your quadrilaterals
   (a) use a protractor to measure the size of each angle
   (b) add the four angles together.

? What do the four angles of a quadrilateral add up to?

*I can draw a quadrilateral
with 4 acute angles.*

Samir

? Is Samir right?

Exercise

1 Work out the missing angles in these triangles and quadrilaterals.

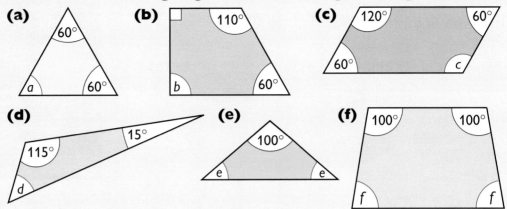

(a) 60° / a / 60°

(b) 110° / b / 60°

(c) 120° / 60° / 60° / c

(d) 15° / 115° / d

(e) 100° / e / e

(f) 100° / 100° / f / f

SU

2 Look at these pictures.

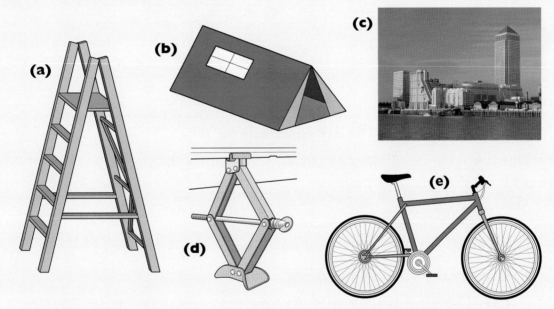

(a)

(b)

(c)

(d)

(e)

Find and name all the different triangles and quadrilaterals in each picture.

Activity   This is a parallelogram.
Use a protractor to measure
the angles of the parallelogram.

?   **What do you notice?**

Draw some more parallelograms and measure their angles.

?   **What have you found out about the angles of
a parallelogram?**

Polygons, angles and drawing

This famous building is called the Pentagon.

 Why is it called this? What happens there?

  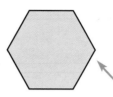 

> *2-D shapes with straight sides are called polygons.*

> *If all the sides and angles of a polygon are equal, the shape is a regular polygon.*

 What names are given to polygons with 6 sides? 8 sides? 10 sides?

Task

A **regular hexagon** has six equal sides.

There are six equal angles at the centre of the hexagon.

 What do all the angles at the centre add up to?

This equation gives the size of each angle at the centre. $360° \div 6 = 60°$

1 Construct a regular hexagon.

   (a) Use a protractor to make the angles at the centre.

   (b) Use compasses to mark the end of each line.

2 **(a)** Now work out the angle at the centre of an **octagon**.

   (b) Construct a regular octagon, with each side 5 cm long.

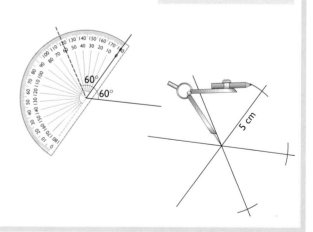

Look at your constructions.

 What sort of triangles have you drawn in each polygon?

Exercise

1 Which of the polygons are regular and which are not?

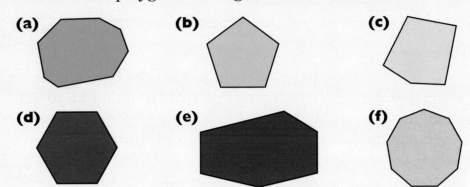

(a)   **(b)**   **(c)**

(d)   **(e)**   **(f)**

2 **(a)** Work out the angle at the centre of a regular **pentagon**.

(b) Construct a regular pentagon.

A pentagon has 5 sides.

3 **(a)** What is the special name for a regular quadrilateral?

(b) What is the special name for a regular triangle?

Activity   Copy and complete the table.

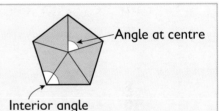

(a) Name the regular polygons with the number of sides given.

(b) Work out

(i) the angle at the centre

(ii) the interior angle.

The first shape has been done for you.

Number of sides	Name	Angle at centre	Interior angle
3	equilateral triangle	120°	60°
4			
5			
6			
8			
9			
10			
12			

Finishing off

Now that you have finished this chapter you should:

- be able to measure and draw angles accurately
- know and use the fact that angles on a **straight line** add up to 180°
- know and use the fact that angles in a **full turn** add up to 360°
- know and use the fact that angles in a **triangle** add up to 180°
- know and use the fact that angles in a **quadrilateral** add up to 360°
- know the names of common polygons
- be able to construct regular polygons by working out angle facts.

Review exercise

1 Look at these diagrams.
Work out the size of the missing angle in each diagram.

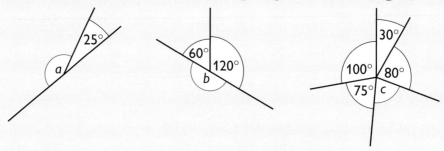

2 **(a)** What is special about a **regular** polygon?
   (b) Which of these polygons are regular?

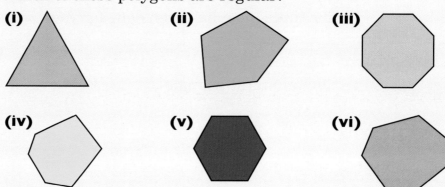

3 A regular polygon has 12 sides.
   (a) Work out the angle at the centre of the polygon.
   (b) Use a ruler and protractor to construct the polygon.
      The sides of the polygon can be any length.
   (c) Find out the special name for a 12-sided polygon.

4 Kieran is a tour guide at a castle.

He draws a plan of the castle to help the visitors.

Look at the plan.

(a) What shape is the plan?

(b) The angle *a* is acute. What are the special names for the other marked angles?

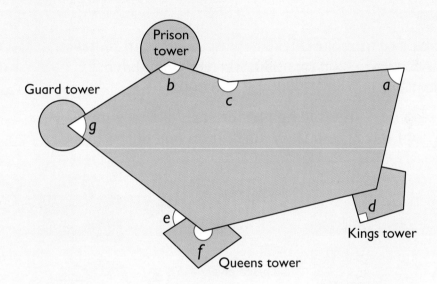

Activity This fairground ride is based on a regular polygon.

Draw the plan of the ride with all the angles constructed accurately.

The plan is the view from above.

Design your own ride based on any regular polygon.

Directed numbers review

(?) **Look at this line showing land heights.**
Sea level is at 0 metres.

What are the missing numbers?

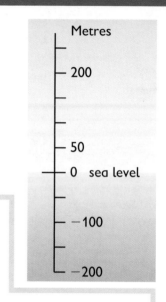

Metres

200

50

0   sea level

−100

−200

Task

1 Draw two number lines showing heights in metres.
One is from −200 to +250, like the one above.
The other is from −5000 to +15 000.

2 Decide on a suitable height for each of these items.
Write it down, and then mark it on one of the lines.

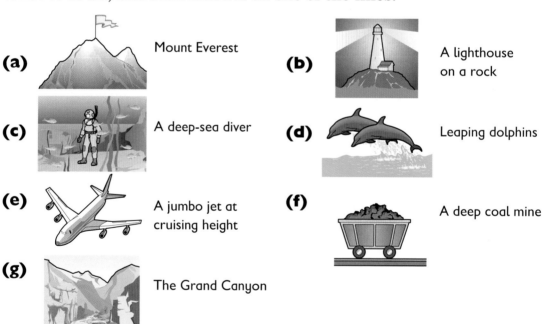

(a) Mount Everest

(b) A lighthouse on a rock

(c) A deep-sea diver

(d) Leaping dolphins

(e) A jumbo jet at cruising height

(f) A deep coal mine

(g) The Grand Canyon

3 Now put in some items of your own on each number line.

(?) **What is**
(a) 4 more than 3   **(b)** 4 less than 3
(c) 4 more than −3   **(d)** 4 less than −3?

(?) **How do you show these on a number line?**

Exercise

1 Put these heights in order, the lowest first.
0 m, −1 m, 2 m, 10 m, 105 m, −12 m, −50 m

SU

2 **(a)** Copy and complete this number line.

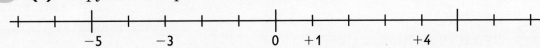

(b) Work these out. Show your work on the number line.

(i) $(+5) + (-2)$ **(ii)** $(-5) + (+2)$ **(iii)** $(+5) + (+2)$

(iv) $(-5) + (-2)$ **(v)** $(-3) + (+6)$ **(vi)** $(+6) + (-4)$

(vii) $(0) + (-3)$ **(viii)** $(+6) + (0)$ **(ix)** $(-3) + (-1)$

(x) $(-2) + (+2)$

3 Brackets are often left out.
So $(+1) - (+2)$ is written as $+1 - 2$, and the answer is -1.
Work these out.

(a) $+3 - 2$ **(b)** $(-5) + 3$ **(c)** $10 + 2$

(d) $(-7) - 2$ **(e)** $(-3) + 9$ **(f)** $(-6) + 4 - 3$

(g) $0 - 5 + 5$ **(h)** $(-6) + 0 + 6$ **(i)** $(-4) + 1 + 10$

(j) $7 - 7 - 4$

SU

4 Avonford and Dartfield are having a tug-of-war.

To win, one team must pull the other a distance of 3 m.

Show the progress of Avonford on a number line.

Avonford
West ←

Dartfield
East →

(a) East 1 m **(b)** West 2 m

(c) East 3 m **(d)** West 4 m

(e) East 3 m **(f)** West 5 m

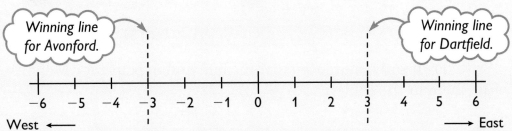

Winning line for Avonford.

Winning line for Dartfield.

West ⟵

⟶ East

Which team wins the tug-of-war?

Addition and subtraction

Harry has £50 in his bank account.
He pays for a DVD player by credit card.
It costs £80.

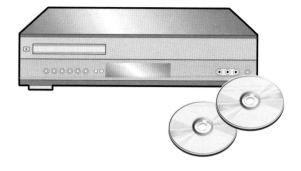

 What is his bank balance?

Harry's uncle gives him £35 for his birthday.
He puts this into his bank account.

 What is his bank balance now?

Task

At the start of June, Megan has £15 in her account.
On 5th June she spends £2 on chocolates.
On 7th June she buys a CD for £17.
On 11th June, her Dad gives her £25 for her birthday.
She goes out with her friend that evening and spends £20 on a meal.

1 Copy and fill in this table.
Find out if her bank balance is negative or positive.

Date	Notes	Income (£)	Expense (£)	Balance (£)
1st June				15.00
5th June	Chocolates		2.00	

2 Write down some more items of income and expense for Megan.
Put them in the table.

 What is the meaning of 'in the red'?
Do banks still use red ink?

Exercise

1 Work out these amounts.

(a) $3 - 1$ **(b)** $-13 + 1$ **(c)** $-23 - 10$

(d) $20 - 41$ **(e)** $-7 + 120$ **(f)** $-7 + (-3)$

(g) $15 - 0 - 7$ **(h)** $0 + 25 - 36$ **(i)** $-12 + 14 - 0$

(j) $26 - 40 + 13$ **(k)** $-26 + 40 - 13$ **(l)** $-26 - 40 - 13$

2 Look at this display of the floors in a hotel.

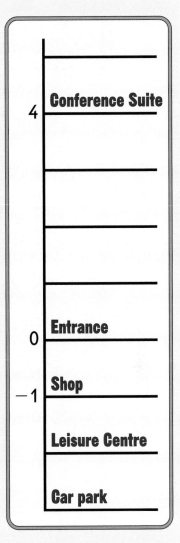

Michelle is in the conference suite on floor 4. Ali is in the shop on the basement floor (-1). The entrance is on the ground floor (0).

(a) How many floors are there from

   (i) Michelle to the ground floor

   (ii) Ali to the ground floor

   (iii) Michelle to Ali?

(b) Michelle and Ali go down to the leisure centre.

   (i) How many floors does Michelle go down?

   (ii) How many floors does Ali go down?

(c) After the leisure centre, Ali goes up 6 floors.
Where is she now?

(d) Michelle goes down to the car park.

   (i) What is the number of that floor?

   (ii) How many floors are there now from Michelle to Ali?

Activity   Find out which is the highest building in the world.

Finishing off

Now that you have finished this chapter you should be able to:
● Add and subtract negative numbers.

Review exercise

1 **(a)** Work out these additions.

    (i) $9 + (-5)$ **(ii)** $(-12) + (-14)$

    (iii) $(-6) + (-7)$ **(iv)** $(-2) + 0$

    (v) $0 + (-5)$ **(vi)** $(-10) + 0 + (-15)$

(b) Work out these subtractions.

    (i) $9 - 5$ **(ii)** $(-12) - 14$

    (iii) $(-6) - 7$ **(iv)** $(-2) - 0$

    (v) $0 - 5$ **(vi)** $(-10) - 0 - 15$

2 Look at this diagram of a cliff.

(a) How far above the water surface is the cliff top?

(b) How far below the water surface is the bottom of the sea?

(c) What is the distance between the cliff top and the bottom of the sea?

Wayne dives 10 metres into the water.

(d) How near to the bottom of the sea does he get?

(e) How far is the cliff top from the bottom of his dive?

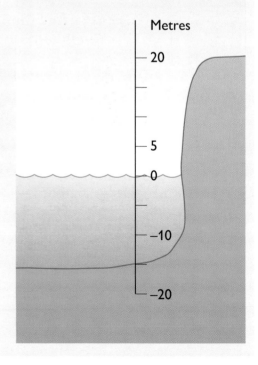

3 **(a)** Sophie's bank account is £10 overdrawn.
She pays in £25.
What is her new balance?

(b) Pete's bank account is £25 in credit.
He draws out £30.
What is the new balance?

(c) Jack's bank account is £27 overdrawn.
He takes out £15.
What is his new balance?

4 Look at this table of temperatures taken in Avonford during one week in February.

Monday	Tuesday	Wednesday	Thursday	Friday	Saturday	Sunday
5 °C	2 °C	−1 °C	−2 °C	0 °C	1 °C	2 °C

(a) What is the difference in temperature between
(i) Monday and Wednesday
(ii) Wednesday and Thursday
(iii) Thursday and Friday
(iv) Friday and Sunday?

(b) What is the difference between the lowest temperature and the highest?

5 The clock in Christina's kitchen gains 4 minutes every day.
She sets it 12 minutes slow on Sunday at noon.

(a) Is it still slow at noon on Monday? By how much?

(b) Is it fast or slow after 2 days? By how much?

(c) Copy and fill in this table.

Noon	Monday	Tuesday	Wednesday	Thursday	Friday
Fast or slow					
How much					

(d) When does the clock show the correct time?

9 Sequences and number machines

Sequences and number machines review

This is John's number machine.

Input ⟶ ×3 ⟶ +1 ⟶ Output

His inputs are the numbers 1 to 10. The outputs make a sequence:

4   7   10   13   ☐ ☐ ☐ ☐ ☐ ☐

? Complete the sequence.

? What are the differences in the outputs? Why is this?

Task

John thinks of some more number machines.

Do the following for each sequence.
(i) Work out the differences.
(ii) Fill in the missing numbers.
(iii) Copy the number machine and fill in the boxes.

Input ⟶ × ⟶ ☐ ⟶ Output

(a)   3   5   7   9   ☐   ☐

(b)   4   6   8   ☐   ☐   ☐

(c)   ☐   ☐   ☐   14   17   20

(d)   ☐   12   ☐   ☐   27   32

Jo

I have thought of another number machine. Do you know what it is?

Input	1	2	3	4	5	6
Output	2	5	10	17	26	37

? What is Jo's number machine?

Exercise

1 Use the numbers 1, 2, 3 up to 6 as inputs for these number machines. Write the outputs as sequences.

(a) Input ⟶ × 3 ⟶ + 15 ⟶ Output

(b) Input ⟶ × 8 ⟶ − 7 ⟶ Output

(c) Input ⟶ × 11 ⟶ + 19 ⟶ Output

2 Look at this number machine.

Input ⟶ × 8 ⟶ + 3 ⟶ Output

Which of these sequences comes from this machine?
What are the missing numbers?

(a) 8   16   24   32

(b) 11   14   17   20

(c) 11   19   27   35

3 Look at this sequence.

11   17   23   29

Which number machine below produces it?
What are the missing numbers?

(a) Input ⟶ × 5 ⟶ + 6 ⟶ Output

(b) Input ⟶ × 6 ⟶ + 5 ⟶ Output

(c) Input ⟶ × 10 ⟶ + 1 ⟶ Output

Investigation

Choose a number between 0 and 10. Use it as Input for this number machine.

Input ⟶ + 5 ⟶ × 2 ⟶ − 10 ⟶ ÷ 2 ⟶ Output

What do you notice?
Does the same thing always happen? Explain why.

Generating sequences

Look at these windmill patterns.

 What patterns can you see in the diagrams?

  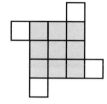

Windmill 1   Windmill 2   Windmill 3

Task

1 Draw the next 2 windmills.

2 Copy and complete this table.

Number of windmill	1	2	3	4	5
Number of white squares	4	4			
Number of coloured squares	1	4			

3 Look at the number of white squares. What do you notice?

4 Look at the number of coloured squares. What type of numbers are these?

5 **(a)** How many white squares does windmill 6 have?
   (b) How many coloured squares does windmill 6 have?

6 **(a)** Draw windmill 6.
   (b) Count the coloured squares and the white squares. Write down the numbers.

7 Now check your answers for question 5. Say if you were correct.

Think about windmill 10.

 How many white squares does it have? Why is this?

 How many coloured squares does it have? Why is this?

 Can you make a windmill with exactly 404 squares?

Exercise

Look at these diagrams.

Diagram 1   Diagram 2   Diagram 3

1 Draw the next 2 diagrams.

2 Copy and complete the table.

Number of diagram	1	2	3	4	5
Number of purple squares	4				
Number of blue squares	1				

3 Look at the numbers of mauve squares. Describe these numbers.

4 Look at the number of blue squares. Describe these numbers.

5 Think about diagram 6.
   (a) How many mauve squares does it have?
   (b) How many blue squares does it have?

6 Now draw diagram 6. Count the mauve squares and the blue squares.

7 Think about diagram 10.
   (a) How many mauve squares does it have?
   (b) How many blue squares does it have?

Investigation

Look at these game boards. Draw the next 2 boards.

Write down the numbers of yellow and pink squares on each board. What do you notice?

A full size draughts board is 8 squares by 8 squares.
How many black squares does it have? How many white squares?

Sequences and spreadsheets

Sophie is buying a mobile phone.

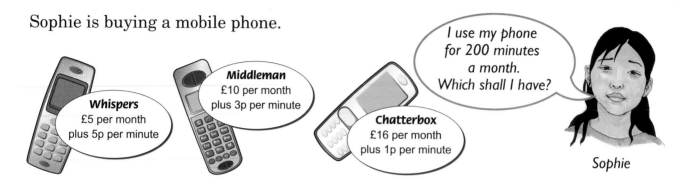

Whispers
£5 per month
plus 5p per minute

Middleman
£10 per month
plus 3p per minute

Chatterbox
£16 per month
plus 1p per minute

I use my phone for 200 minutes a month. Which shall I have?

Sophie

Look at this spreadsheet for Whispers.

	A	B	C	D	E	F	G	H	I	J	K
1	Number of minutes in one month	50	100	150	200	250	300	350	400	450	500
2	Whispers tariff monthly cost										
3											

In here type the formula
*=B1*0.05+5*
Then press Enter.

? Explain this formula.

Task

1 Set up the spreadsheet for Whispers.
Copy and paste the formula to work out the other costs.

2 What does this tariff cost Sophie for a month?

3 Add another row to the table for the Middleman tariff.
   (a) What formula do you need to type in?
   (b) Put in the formula.
   (c) Copy and paste the formula to work out the other costs.
   (d) What does the Middleman tariff cost Sophie for a month?

4 Now add and complete a row for the Chatterbox tariff.

? Which of the tariffs is best for Sophie?

Pete uses his mobile a lot.

? How many minutes per month does he use his mobile?

The Chatterbox tariff is best for me.

Pete

Exercise

1

	A	B
1	9	
2		

Karl puts the formula =A1*3+20 here and then presses Enter.

What number does the computer show?

2 A formula is put into cell A2 and then copied across.

	A	B	C	D	E	F
1	1	2	3	4	5	6
2	12	22	32	42	52	62

The formula is =A1*10+2

No, the formula is =A1*2+10

Samir

Who is correct?

Michelle

3 Meena is putting a formula into a spreadsheet. She has 3 tries but they do not work. What has she done wrong each time?

(a) | A1*3+2 |

(b) | =A1x3+2 |

(c) | =1A*3+2 |

4

Rental
£3 plus
50 pence for
every extra day

Kim creates this table on a spreadsheet. Look at it carefully.

	A	B	C	D	E	F
1	Number of days the DVD is rented	1	2	3	4	5
2	Cost of rental	£3	£53	£103	£153	£203

Kim has made a mistake.

(a) How do you know? **(b)** What mistake has she made?

Finishing off

Now that you have finished this chapter you should be able to:

- use number machines
- investigate patterns
- make a table in a spreadsheet.

Review exercise

1

£3 PER HOUR ON THE RINK PLUS £2 FOR SKATE HIRE

I am going for 1 hour.

I've got 3 hours before my mum picks me up.

I am going to stay for 2 hours.

Wanda Sam Terry

(a) How much does Sam pay? Show your workings.

(b) How much do Wanda and Terry pay each? Show your workings.

The cost can be worked out using this number machine.

| Number of hours | → | number of hours × ☐ | → | + ☐ for skate hire | → | Cost |

(c) Copy and complete the number machine.

The skating rink has a table to help the receptionist work out the costs.

Number of hours	1	2	3	4	5	6
Cost (including skate hire)						

(d) Copy and complete the table.
Use the number machine to help you.

(e) What patterns are there in your answers?

The table can be made using a spreadsheet.
A formula is put in to calculate the cost.

(f) Which one of these formulae is correct?

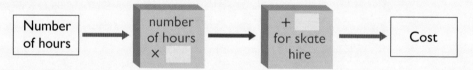

=A1*2+3   =A1*3+2   =A1*5

2 Look at these diagrams.

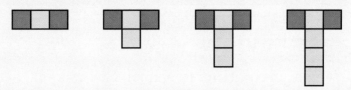

The total number of squares is worked out using this number machine.

(a) What goes in the box? Why?

(b) What is the total number of squares when there are 9 blue squares?

The total number of squares is 20.

(c) How many pink squares are there?

(d) How many blue squares are there?

A table is set up in a spreadsheet to work out the answers.

	A	B	C	D	E
1	Number of blue squares	1	2	3	4
2	Total number of squares				

(e) What formula is put into cell B2?

Investigation

Think of a number between 1 and 9. Write it down.
Subtract your number from 10. Write down the answer.
Subtract your answer from 10. Write down your answer. ... and so on ...

Describe the sequence you have made.

Percentages review

Lucy does a survey at break time in school. She asks 20 students what drink they have for break. Here are her results.

Pipsy	IIII III	8
7 Down	IIII II	
Sunshine Delicious	IIII	
Another drink	I	

Lucy calculates that 40% of the students drink Pipsy. Look at her working.

$\frac{8}{20}$ pupils drink Pipsy: $\frac{8}{20} = \frac{40}{100} = 40\%$

 Explain her working.

 Work out the percentages for the other drinks. Show your working.

Task

Lucy also asks the same 20 students what they eat at break time. Look at her results.

1 Work out the percentage for each snack. Show your working.

2 Draw a chart to show Lucy's results more clearly.

Crisps	IIII I
chocolate bar	IIII
fruit	IIII
biscuits or cake	III
sandwich	II
another snack	

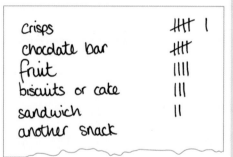
There are 1200 people in my school. 40% of 1200 is 480, so exactly 480 people in my school prefer to drink Pipsy.

Lucy

 Is Lucy right?

One break time, Lucy counts the number of students who use the school tuck shop. She counts 217.

  How do you work this out as a percentage of all the students?

Exercise

1   50 students are asked to name their
    favourite winter sport.
    Work out the percentage that prefers
    each sport. Show your working.

Football	21
Hockey	13
Rugby	9
Gymnastics	5
Netball	2

2   A class has 25 students.
    7 go to Spain for a
    holiday.
    What percentage is this?

3   Karl tries to calculate 16 out
    of 35 as a percentage.
    Which of these is correct?

(a) $\frac{16}{100} \times 35$

(b) $\frac{16}{35} \times 100$

(c) $\frac{35}{16} \times 100$

(d) $\frac{35}{100} \times 16$

4   Alan does the following calculation.
    His answer is wrong.
    How can you tell?

96 out of 120 = 32%

5   What is the approximate percentage of
    fruit and nuts?

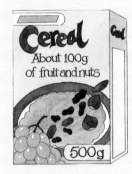

About 100g
of fruit and nuts

500g

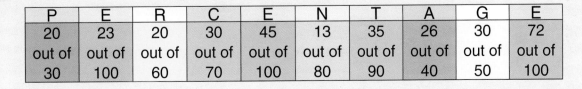

Activity On a copy of the chart, shade in all the answers over 50% to
make a word. Look carefully at each question. Sometimes you do
not have to work out the answer!

P	E	R	C	E	N	T	A	G	E
20	23	20	30	45	13	35	26	30	72
out of	out of	out of	out of	out of	out of	out of	out of	out of	out of
30	100	60	70	100	80	90	40	50	100

Percentage of an amount

Amy wants to find 65% of 120. This is what she writes.

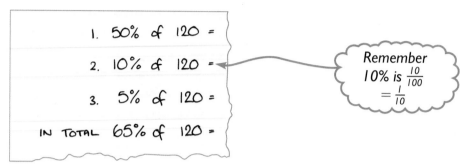

1. 50% of 120 =

2. 10% of 120 =

3. 5% of 120 =

IN TOTAL 65% of 120 =

Remember
10% is $\frac{10}{100}$
$= \frac{1}{10}$

? What are her answers?

? Explain her working.

Task

1 Copy the percentage network below.
Use the number in the coloured circle. Complete all the white circles.

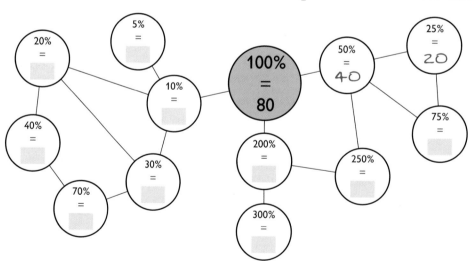

5%
=

20%
=

50%
=
40

25%
=
20

100%
=
80

10%
=

75%
=

40%
=

200%
=

250%
=

30%
=

70%
=

300%
=

2 Now work out the following percentages. Use your completed network.

(a) 60% of 80   **(b)** 90% of 80   **(c)** 35% of 80

(d) 150% of 80   **(e)** 285% of 80

? How can you find $2\frac{1}{2}$% of 80 using the network?

? What about 15% of 160?

Exercise

1. Mercy wants to find 160% of 30. Complete Mercy's workings.

1. 100% of 30 =
2. 50% of 30 =
3. 10% of 30 =

IN TOTAL 160% of 30 =

2. In this box of chocolates, 40% are made with milk chocolate. How many milk chocolates are there?

3. (a) How many grams of cocoa are there in the chocolate bar?

   (b) There are 20 g of sugar. What percentage is sugar?

   (c) The rest is vegetable fat. What percentage is fat?

4. 60% of the human body is water. Tracey weighs 70 kg. Work out the weight of water in her body.

5. Gilly's father asks her to find a percentage of 20. Her answer is 8. What percentage has she found?

   50%   60%   40%   25%   100%

6. Frank tries to find 40% of 86. His answer is 61. How do you know he has made a mistake. You do not need to do any calculation.

Activity   Draw your own 'percentage network' for the number 200. Find as many percentages as you can.

Percentage increase or decrease

This is where I work on a Saturday. I earn £4 an hour. I work 5 hours.

Harry

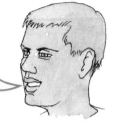

All my staff get a 10% pay increase from today.

Harry's boss

Harry works out his new pay like this.

Old pay	£4.00
10% rise	£0.40
New pay	£4.40

 Explain his working.

 How much does he earn on a Saturday after the pay rise?

? He works for 50 Saturdays a year.
How much money does he earn in a year?

Task

All the staff at the sports shop get a 10% pay increase. Work out the new pay for each employee. Show your working.

Sid
Cleaner
£50 per week

Sarah
Sales assistant
£6 per hour

Sam
Senior sales assistant
£8 per hour

Sharon
Manageress
£15 000 pa

There is a sale in the sports shop.

 How much are the trainers decreased by?

 How much are the trainers in the sale?

15% off were £40 Now

Exercise

1 Increase the prices of these items by 10%. Show your working.

(a)

(b)

(c)

2 Decrease the prices of these items by 20%. Show your working.

(a)

(b)

(c)

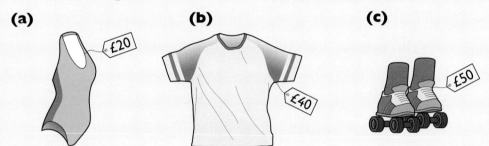

3 Christina increases 50 by 10%. Her answer is 60. How do you know she is wrong?

4 Full fat cheese has 120 g of fat. How much does the low fat cheese have?

Low Fat Cheese
25% less fat than
full fat cheese

5 Andy decreases 40 by a percentage. His answer is 30. What percentage has he used?

7%   10%   25%   30%

Activity Decrease each number. Shade in all the answers under 100. The shaded answers spell another word.

D	E	C	R	E	A	S	E	S
110	150	120	120	130	200	80	200	150
by	by	by	by	by	by	by	by	by
10%	10%	15%	20%	30%	50%	5%	40%	50%

Finishing off

Now that you have finished this chapter you should be able to:

- work out percentages
- find a percentage of an amount
- increase or decrease a number by a percentage.

Review exercise

1 40 people are asked what fruit they like best.
The results are shown in the pie chart.

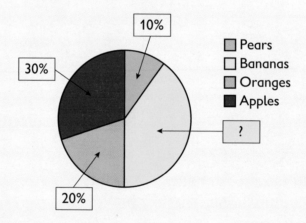

(a) What percentage of the people prefer bananas?

(b) How many people prefer pears?

(c) How many people prefer apples or oranges?

2

I put £200 into the Countrywide Building Society, I got £12 interest.

Granny

I put £240 into the Mat East Bank. I got £12 interest as well.

Stuart

(a) Who got the better rate of interest? Explain your answer.

(b) What percentage interest did Granny get?

3 Copy the diagram and complete the boxes.

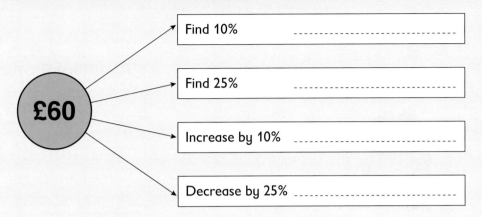

Find 10% ------------------------------

Find 25% ------------------------------

£60

Increase by 10% ------------------------------

Decrease by 25% ------------------------------

4 Samir asks 40 friends 'Do you like the colour of the school uniform?'

25% say 'Yes'.   55% say 'No'.   The rest say 'Don't know'.

(a) What percentage say 'Don't know?'

(b) Copy and fill in the table to show their answers.

	Yes	No	Don't know
Answers			

Activity   Copy and complete the cross-number.

Across
1 50% of 600
2 $\frac{1}{4}$ as a percentage
4 50% of this number is 120
5 87% of 100
6 0.75 as a percentage
7 10% of 620
9 25% of 1000
10 30% of 150
11 Increase 10 by 100%

Down
1 10% of this number is 35
2 20% of 120
3 6 is this percentage of 12
4 Decrease 30 by 10%
5 200% of 425
6 Decrease 1000 by 25%
7 32% of 200
8 Increase 200 by 25%
9 5% of 440

Using brackets

Meena goes ten pin bowling with her friends.

Avonford Bowling
£3.50 per game
£2.00 shoe hire

Special Offer
All drinks £1
Pizza and salad £3

Meena

How much will it cost for 10 people?

Meena writes:

Cost (£) = 10 × 3·50 + 10 × 2 + 10 × 1 + 10 × 3

I can use brackets: Cost (£) = 10 × (3·50 + 2 + 1 + 3)

This is called **factorising**.

? **Why can Meena put the '10' outside the brackets?**
What is the total cost?

Remember to work out what is inside the brackets first.

? **Factorise and then work out these.**
(a) $4 \times 6 + 4 \times 2$
(b) $3 \times 9 + 4 \times 9 - 2 \times 9$

? **How do you write $4 \times 3 + 6 \times 7 - 3 \times 3 - 5 \times 7$ using brackets?**

Task

1 Look at this multiplication grid.
Look at any 2 by 2 square in it.
Add together the opposite corners.
$6 + 12 = 18$
$8 + 9 = 17$

Find the difference between your answers.
$18 - 17 = 1$

×	1	2	3	4
1	1	2	3	4
2	2	4	6	8
3	3	6	9	12
4	4	8	12	16

$2 \times 4 = 8$

Hint: For the yellow square, you are working out
$3 \times 2 + 4 \times 3 - 4 \times 2 - 3 \times 3$

2 (a) Look at 3 more squares.
Does this always happen?
Explain what is happening by using brackets.

(b) Investigate 3 by 3 squares and 4 by 4 squares.
What do you notice?

? Why is it helpful to use brackets?

Exercise

1 Work out the following.

(a) $7 \times (5 + 2)$ (b) $(7 \times 5) + 2$ (c) $3 \times (4 + 6)$

(d) $(3 \times 4) + 6$ (e) $4 \times (9 - 1)$ (f) $(4 \times 9) - 1$

(g) $(3 + 2) \times (5 - 3)$ (h) $3 + (2 \times 5) - 3$ (i) $3 + (2 \times (5 - 3))$

2 Work out the following.

(a) $3 \times (5 + 2 + 9)$ (b) $5 \times (10 + 3 - 6)$

(c) $8 \times (12 + 3 - 10)$ (d) $2 \times (13 + 7 + 3)$

3 (a) Factorise the following.

(i) $4 \times 3 + 4 \times 5$ (ii) $7 \times 3 - 7 \times 2$

(iii) $2 \times 3 + 5 \times 3$ (iv) $4 \times 5 + 5 \times 5$

(v) $4 \times 5 - 3 \times 5$ (vi) $3 \times 2 + 4 \times 2 + 5 \times 2$

(vii) $7 \times 5 + 7 \times 3 - 7 \times 7$ (viii) $9 \times 5 + 9 \times 3 - 9 \times 4$

(b) Work out the value of each part of (a).

4 Jamie plans a trip to the cinema with his friends.
They need to catch the bus and have a meal out.

Avonford Films
Tickets £6

McBurgers
Burgers £2
Fries £1
Mega drink £1.50

Avonford Travel
Return Fare 50p

(a) Write down how to work out the total cost for 7 people.

(b) Write down how to work out the cost using brackets.

(c) Work out how much the trip costs for
    (i) 7   (ii) 10   (iii) 5   (iv) 15 people.

Investigation

Look at the multiplication grid on page 84.
Investigate opposite corners in a rectangle.
Start with a 2 by 3 rectangle.
What is the next size to look at?

Expanding brackets

Mercy is working out the area of this rectangle.

Mercy

I can split it into 2 rectangles.

17 cm

5 cm

10 cm   7 cm

5 cm

Area of a rectangle = length × width
So Area = 17 × 5
= (10 + 7) × 5
= 10 × 5 + 7 × 5

*Mercy has **expanded** the brackets.*

(?) **What is the area of the rectangle?**
Why has using brackets helped?

(?) **Expand these brackets.**
(a) $3 \times (5 + 8)$ **(b)** $(6 - 2) \times 12$ **(c)** $8 \times (100 + 20 + 6)$
How can you check your answers?

Task

1 Find the area of these rectangles.

(a)   20 cm   6 cm
3 cm

(b)   18 cm
6 cm

(c)   34 cm
9 cm

2 For each part **(i)** and **(ii)** below,
   (a) work out the area of the 4 small rectangles
   (b) work out the area of the large rectangle.

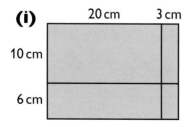

(i)   20 cm   3 cm
10 cm
6 cm

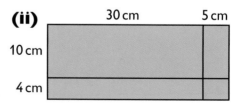

(ii)   30 cm   5 cm
10 cm
4 cm

(?) **How would you expand $(30 + 2) \times (20 + 6)$?**

Exercise

1 Expand the brackets and then work these out.

(a) $5 \times (12 + 4)$ (b) $(20 + 8) \times 2$

(c) $9 \times (40 + 3)$ (d) $(10 + 6) \times 15$

2 Use brackets to work out the following.

(a) $7 \times 24 = 7 \times (20 + 4) = $

(b) 8×14 (c) 9×32 (d) 6×59

(e) 3×128 (f) 5×236 (g) 7×325

3 Work out the areas of these rectangles.

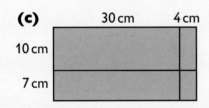

(a) 45 cm, 3 cm

(b) 72 cm, 8 cm

(c) 30 cm, 4 cm, 10 cm, 7 cm

(d) 24 cm, 19 cm

4 Work these out.

(a) 12×15 (b) 14×26 (c) 17×42

5 (a) Write down two different ways of working out the green area.

(b) By expanding the brackets, show that

$8 \times (8 - 5) + 5 \times (8 - 5)$
$= 8 \times 8 - 5 \times 5$

(c) How can you rearrange the green area to show that its area equals $13 \times (8 - 5)$?

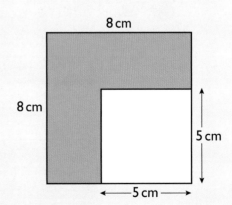

8 cm

8 cm

5 cm

5 cm

Finishing off

Now that you have finished this chapter you should:

● know the meaning of the words **factorise** and **expand**
● be able to use brackets in calculations.

Review exercise

1 Work out the following.

(a) $3 \times (4 + 2)$ **(b)** $(3 \times 4) + 2$

(c) $5 \times (7 - 3)$ **(d)** $(5 \times 7) - 3$

(e) $5 \times (8 + 4 - 3)$ **(f)** $12 \times (4 + 3 - 6)$

(g) $7 + (3 \times 8) - 4$ **(h)** $(7 + 3) \times (8 - 4)$

(i) $7 + (3 \times (8 - 4))$ **(j)** $(7 + 3) \times 8 - 4$

2 **(a)** Factorise the following.

    (i) $5 \times 2 + 5 \times 4$ **(ii)** $4 \times 4 - 4 \times 2$

    (iii) $3 \times 7 + 2 \times 7$ **(iv)** $9 \times 3 + 9 \times 8 - 9 \times 9$

(b) Work out the value of each question in part **(a)**.

3 For each part, expand the brackets and then work out its value.

(a) $7 \times (10 + 5)$ **(b)** $8 \times (30 + 2)$

(c) $9 \times (30 - 1)$ **(d)** $20 \times (8 + 6)$

4 Work out the areas of these rectangles.

(a)

25 cm

4 cm

(b)

34 cm

7 cm

(c)

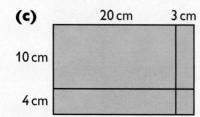

20 cm   3 cm

10 cm

4 cm

(d)

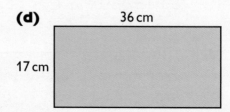

36 cm

17 cm

5 Draw a rectangle or use brackets to help you work out the following.

(a) $6 \times 27 = 6 \times (20 + 7) = $ ▢

(b) 8×15　　　　(c) 7×23　　　　(d) 4×79

(e) 17×12　　　　(f) 23×15　　　　(g) 37×19

SU

6 Avonford Nurseries have these plants in their greenhouses.

> Greenhouse 1:　20 rows of 40 daffodils
> Greenhouse 2:　25 rows of 40 tulips
> Greenhouse 3:　25 rows of 55 roses

(a) Match each question to the correct calculation:

| How many rows of plants have they got altogether? | $(40 \times 25) + (40 \times 20)$ |

$25 - 20$

$(20 \times 40) + 25 \times (40 + 55)$

| How many plants have they got altogether? | $20 + (25 \times 2)$ |

$(20 + 40) + (25 + 40) + (25 + 55)$

| There are more plants in greenhouse 2 than in greenhouse 1. How many more? | $40 + 40 + 55$ |

$40 \times (25 - 20)$

$20 - 25$

| There are more rows of plants in greenhouse 3 than in greenhouse 1. How many more? | $(40 \times 25) - 20$ |

(b) Make up questions to go with these calculations.

(i) $(25 \times 55) + (20 \times 40)$　　　　(ii) $25 \times (55 - 40)$

12 Fractions

Fractions review

Look at the drawings of how Tabby spends her day:

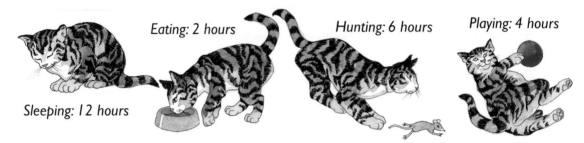

Eating: 2 hours

Hunting: 6 hours

Playing: 4 hours

Sleeping: 12 hours

? How can these times be written as fractions?

? What are the fractions in their simplest form?

Task

Think how you spend a typical school day.
Copy and fill in the table.

Activity	Hours	Fraction	Simplest form
Sleeping			
At school			
Travelling			
Working			
Relaxing			
Total:			

? The fractions $\frac{8}{12}$ and $\frac{2}{3}$ are **equivalent**.
What does this mean?
What other fractions are equivalent to $\frac{8}{12}$?

? A lion spends $\frac{2}{3}$ of one day sleeping.
How many hours is this?

Exercise

1 You need six copies of this clock.
On each clock shade the fraction of an hour.

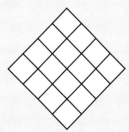

(a) $\frac{1}{4}$ hour   (b) $\frac{1}{3}$ hour   (c) $\frac{1}{6}$ hour

(d) $\frac{1}{2}$ hour   (e) $\frac{2}{3}$ hour   (f) $\frac{1}{12}$ hour

2 Write these fractions in their simplest form.

(a) $\frac{4}{16}$ (b) $\frac{6}{8}$ (c) $\frac{9}{12}$ (d) $\frac{11}{22}$ (e) $\frac{12}{18}$ (f) $\frac{14}{21}$

3 Copy these and fill in the spaces.

(a) $\frac{1}{10} = \frac{}{20}$ (b) $\frac{2}{5} = \frac{}{20}$ (c) $\frac{1}{4} = \frac{}{20}$

(d) $\frac{3}{5} = \frac{}{20}$ (e) $\frac{3}{4} = \frac{}{20}$ (f) $\frac{3}{10} = \frac{}{20}$

4 Lucy, Michelle and Ali share £36.
Lucy gets £18.   Michelle gets £12.   Ali gets £6.
What fraction does each get? Write them in their simplest form.

5 Tim, Mark and Humza share £30.
Tim gets $\frac{1}{3}$.   Mark gets $\frac{2}{5}$.   Humza gets $\frac{1}{6}$.
How much does each get?
How much is left over? What fraction is left over?

6 Copy these and fill in the spaces.

(a) $\frac{1}{2} = \frac{3}{} = \frac{}{14}$ (b) $\frac{1}{3} = \frac{}{9} = \frac{5}{}$ (c) $\frac{1}{4} = \frac{}{8} = \frac{6}{}$

(d) $\frac{2}{3} = \frac{4}{} = \frac{}{12}$ (e) $\frac{3}{4} = \frac{}{16} = \frac{24}{}$ (f) $\frac{2}{5} = \frac{8}{} = \frac{}{15}$

Activity

1 Copy and colour each of these shapes. Exactly $\frac{1}{4}$ of each shape must be each of red, blue, yellow and green.

  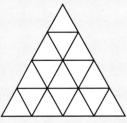

2 Think of 10 fractions which are equivalent to $\frac{1}{2}$ and write them down.
You may only use digits 1, 2, 4.
For example, $\frac{111}{222}$ and $\frac{21}{42}$.
All the numbers must be smaller than 1000.

Adding and subtracting fractions

Megan

? What is $\frac{1}{4} + \frac{1}{4}$?

? How long does it take Megan to get ready for school?

? How did you work out the answer?

Megan writes this.

? Explain what Megan has done.

$$\frac{1}{4} + \frac{1}{2} + \frac{1}{4}$$

$$\frac{1}{4} + \frac{2}{4} + \frac{1}{4}$$

$$\frac{4}{4}$$

$$1$$

| Shower: $\frac{1}{4}$ hour |
| Get dressed: $\frac{1}{2}$ hour |
| Eat breakfast: $\frac{1}{4}$ hour |

Task

Copy and complete this table.

Fraction	Equivalent fraction	Question	Equivalent question	Adding	Simplest form
$\frac{1}{2}$	$\frac{2}{4}$	$\frac{1}{2} + \frac{1}{4}$	$\frac{2}{4} + \frac{1}{4}$	$\frac{3}{4}$	$\frac{3}{4}$
$\frac{1}{6}$	$\frac{\ }{12}$	$\frac{1}{6} + \frac{1}{12}$		$\frac{3}{12}$	$\frac{1}{4}$
$\frac{3}{4}$	$\frac{\ }{8}$	$\frac{3}{4} + \frac{1}{8}$			
$\frac{1}{3}$	$\frac{\ }{6}$	$\frac{1}{3} + \frac{1}{6}$			
$\frac{2}{3}$	$\frac{\ }{6}$	$\frac{1}{6} + \frac{2}{3}$			
$\frac{1}{2}$	$\frac{\ }{8}$	$\frac{3}{8} + \frac{1}{2}$			
$\frac{3}{4}$	$\frac{\ }{12}$	$\frac{3}{4} + \frac{1}{12}$			
$\frac{1}{4}$	$\frac{\ }{8}$	$\frac{1}{4} + \frac{5}{8}$			

? How do you work out $\frac{1}{4} + \frac{1}{3}$?

? What happens when you work out $\frac{1}{2} + \frac{3}{4}$?

? How do you work out $\frac{1}{2} - \frac{1}{6}$?

Exercise

1 Match the answers to the additions.

Additions   **Answers**

$\frac{1}{4}+\frac{1}{4}$ $\frac{1}{2}+\frac{1}{4}$ $\frac{2}{3}$ $1\frac{1}{2}$

$\frac{1}{3}+\frac{1}{3}$ $\frac{5}{12}+\frac{2}{12}$ $\frac{7}{12}$ 1

$\frac{2}{3}+\frac{1}{3}$ $\frac{3}{4}+\frac{3}{4}$ $\frac{3}{4}$ $\frac{1}{2}$

2 Look at the addition $\frac{4}{18}+\frac{5}{18}=\frac{9}{18}=\frac{1}{2}$

Write down five more additions with answer $\frac{1}{2}$.

3 **(a)** Fill in the blank spaces for these equivalent fractions.

    (i) $\frac{1}{5}=\frac{\ \ }{10}=\frac{\ \ }{20}$ **(ii)** $\frac{2}{5}=\frac{\ \ }{10}=\frac{\ \ }{20}$

  (b) Use your answers to work these out.

    (i) $\frac{1}{10}+\frac{3}{10}$ **(ii)** $\frac{1}{5}+\frac{2}{5}$ **(iii)** $\frac{2}{5}+\frac{3}{5}$

    (iv) $\frac{1}{5}+\frac{1}{10}$ **(v)** $\frac{3}{10}-\frac{1}{5}$ **(vi)** $\frac{3}{10}+\frac{2}{5}$

    (vii) $\frac{1}{5}-\frac{1}{20}$ **(viii)** $\frac{7}{20}+\frac{2}{5}$ **(ix)** $\frac{2}{5}-\frac{7}{20}$

4 What fraction of this square is
  (a) blue
  (b) green
  (c) red
  (d) white?

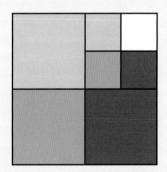

Activity

Look at how Megan's brother Guy spends time getting ready for school.

How long does he take? Is he quicker than Megan?

Time in shower: $\frac{1}{12}$ hour

Time to get dressed: $\frac{1}{4}$ hour

Time to eat breakfast: $\frac{1}{3}$ hour

Guy

Finishing off

Now that you have finished this chapter you should be able to:

- write fractions in their simplest form
- find equivalent fractions
- add and subtract fractions.

Review exercise

1 Copy this table.

$\dfrac{2}{4}$	$\dfrac{8}{12}$	$\dfrac{9}{27}$	$\dfrac{5}{10}$
$\dfrac{2}{6}$	$\dfrac{15}{20}$	$\dfrac{6}{8}$	$\dfrac{3}{12}$
$\dfrac{6}{10}$	$\dfrac{9}{12}$	$\dfrac{12}{16}$	$\dfrac{3}{9}$
$\dfrac{7}{14}$	$\dfrac{11}{33}$	$\dfrac{4}{16}$	$\dfrac{14}{28}$

Colour all the fractions that are equivalent to $\frac{1}{2}$ in red.

Colour all the fractions that are equivalent to $\frac{1}{3}$ in blue.

Colour all the fractions that are equivalent to $\frac{3}{4}$ in yellow.

Write the other fractions in their simplest form.

2 Write these fractions in their simplest form.

(a) $\dfrac{9}{18}$ **(b)** $\dfrac{3}{15}$ **(c)** $\dfrac{12}{16}$

(d) $\dfrac{4}{6}$ **(e)** $\dfrac{15}{20}$ **(f)** $\dfrac{7}{28}$

3 £48 is shared between Wayne, Andy and John.

Wayne gets £16. Andy gets £12. John gets the rest.

What fraction does each get?

Write the fractions in their simplest form.

4 £60 is shared between Jo, Sophie and Meena.

Jo gets $\frac{1}{2}$. Sophie gets $\frac{1}{3}$.

How much money does each get?
How much is left for Meena? What fraction does Meena get?

5 Work these out.

(a) $\frac{3}{8} + \frac{5}{8}$ (b) $\frac{2}{5} + \frac{3}{5}$ (c) $\frac{2}{9} + \frac{7}{9}$

(d) Write down three more additions with answer 1.

6 Write the answers to these additions in the simplest form.

(a) $\frac{3}{11} + \frac{4}{11}$ (b) $\frac{1}{7} + \frac{5}{7}$ (c) $\frac{2}{9} + \frac{1}{9}$

(d) $\frac{3}{8} + \frac{3}{8}$ (e) $\frac{3}{12} + \frac{5}{12}$ (f) $\frac{9}{20} + \frac{7}{20}$

7 (a) Fill in the blank spaces for these equivalent fractions.

$\frac{1}{2} = \frac{}{4} = \frac{}{8}$

(b) Use your answers to work these out.

(i) $\frac{1}{2} + \frac{1}{4}$ (ii) $\frac{3}{4} + \frac{1}{4}$ (iii) $\frac{3}{4} - \frac{1}{4}$

(iv) $\frac{1}{2} + \frac{3}{8}$ (v) $\frac{7}{8} - \frac{1}{2}$ (vi) $\frac{1}{2} - \frac{1}{8}$

8 (a) Find (i) $\frac{1}{2}$ of 20 (ii) $\frac{1}{4}$ of 40 (iii) $\frac{1}{6}$ of 60

(b) Fill in the blank. $\frac{1}{2}$ of 100 = $\frac{1}{4}$ of

9 (a) Look at these fractions. $\frac{1}{2}$ $\frac{1}{3}$ $\frac{5}{6}$

0 $\qquad\qquad\qquad\qquad$ $\underset{\frac{1}{2}}{\uparrow}$ $\qquad\qquad\qquad\qquad$ 1

Copy the number line and mark each fraction on it.
The first one is done for you.

(b) Copy these and fill in the missing numbers.

(i) $\frac{2}{12} = \frac{}{6}$ (ii) $\frac{1}{2} = \frac{12}{}$ (iii) $\frac{1}{} = \frac{6}{24}$

Picture by numbers

Ask your teacher for a copy of the picture opposite of a well-known character. Answer these clues to colour the picture.

A There are 8 kilometres to 5 miles. How many kilometres in 15 miles?

B What is the area of a triangle with base = 12 and height = 6?

C Count how many of the following are 3-D shapes. Cylinder, cuboid, square, sphere, hexagon, pyramid, cube, triangle, circle, rectangle, line.

D The pie chart shows what some girls in Year 9 like for tea.
12 like vegetarian.
How many like fish?

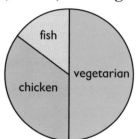

E Share out 60 marbles equally between 4 people. How many each?

F Share out 225 in the ratio 1 : 4. What is the size of the bigger portion?

G Solve $a + 5 = 13$.

H Solve $3n - 20 = 25$.

I What do the angles on a straight line add up to?

J Work out $11 - 7 + 20$.

K Ron's bank account is £20 overdrawn. He pays in £38. What is his new balance?

L How many boxes in the next level down?

M What is 10% of 30?

N What is 15% of 120?

O Work out 7×4, add 6×3 and then subtract 2×5.

P What is $\frac{1}{5}$ of 40?

Answer	Colour	Answer	Colour
3	Purple	5	Green
8	Yellow	15	Blue
18	Brown	24	Red
36	Pink	180	Black

 Who is the picture of?

Co-ordinates review

? What are the co-ordinates of point A?

? In which quadrant is point A?

? What about B and C?
What are their co-ordinates?
Which quadrants are they in?

> Remember the rule:
> across first, then up
> or down.

? What is the special name for the point at (0, 0)?

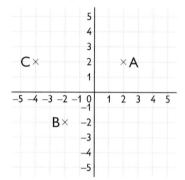

Task

Jack and Harry are playing a game.

Jack throws two dice, one blue
and one red, both numbered from 0 to 5.
They come up 4 (blue) and 5 (red).

Then Jack tosses a coin twice,
first for the blue die
and second for the red die.
The coin lands heads for blue and
tails for red.
Heads is positive and tails is negative.

So, Jack's score is (4, −5).
He marks the point on this grid.

Now it is Harry's turn.

The winner is the first player to get
three points together in a line.

Play the game with a friend.

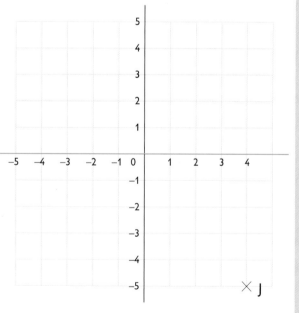

? What do you notice about the co-ordinates of the points in a winning line?

Exercise

1 Look at this grid.
Write down the co-ordinates
for each of the points from
A to F.

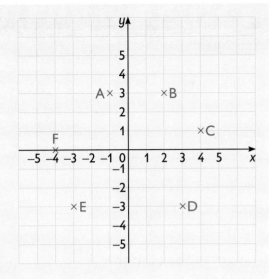

2 Draw a grid with x and y axes from -5 to 5.
On your grid, plot and label these points.

(a) $(3, 5)$ **(b)** $(-2, 1)$ **(c)** $(4, -5)$

(d) $(-3, -1)$ **(e)** $(0, -2)$ **(f)** $(4, 0)$

3 Look at the diagram.

(a) Shape ABCD is a square.
What are the co-ordinates
of point D?

(b) Point E is halfway between
points A and C.
What are the co-ordinates
of point E?

(c) Is point E halfway between
B and D?

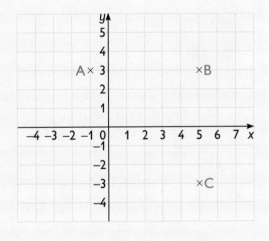

4 Draw a grid with the x axis from -10 to 10 and the y axis
from -8 to 10.
Plot these points, joining them in order as you go along.
$(6, 10), (9, 5), (7, -3), (8, -4), (8, -6), (7, -7), (6, -6), (7, -5),$
$(6, -4), (-4, -2), (-4, -3), (-6, -5), (-7, -4), (-5, -3), (-5, 0),$
$(-7, 1), (-10, 4), (-10, 5), (-9, 5), (-9, 4), (-8, 4), (-8, 3), (-7, 3),$
$(-7, 2), (-6, 2), (-6, 4), (-7, 4), (-7, 5), (-8, 5), (-8, 6), (-9, 6),$
$(-9, 8), (-8, 8), (-8, 7), (-5, 5), (-4, 6), (-3, 5), (-4, 4), (-2, 2),$
$(5, 1), (7, 5), (6, 10)$

What have you drawn?

Tables of values

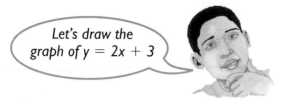

Let's draw the
graph of y = 2x + 3

Karl

Start by making a table
of values.

Choose values for the
x co-ordinates.

Work out the values for
the y co-ordinates.

x	0	1	2	3	4	5
2x	0	2	4	6		
+3	+3	+3	+3	+3	+3	
y = 2x + 3	3	5	7			

 What are the missing values in the table?

Task

Now you can draw the graph of y = 2x + 3.

1 (a) On graph paper, draw an x axis from 0 to 5 and
a y axis from 0 to 15.

(b) Use the x and y co-ordinates from Karl's table
of values to draw the graph of y = 2x + 3.

(c) Join the points with a straight line and label
the line y = 2x + 3.

2 Make tables of values for each of these.

(a) y = 2x + 1   **(b)** y = x + 3   **(c)** y = x + 5

Draw all the graphs on the same axes. Label each
graph.

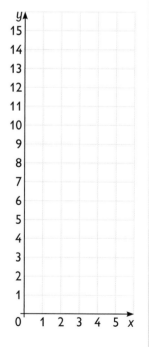

 What shape do the lines make?

 Where do your graphs cross the y axis?

 What do you notice?

Exercise

1 **(a)** Copy and complete this table of values for $y = 2x - 1$.

x	1	2	3	4	5	6
$2x$	2	4				
-1	-1	-1				
$y = 2x - 1$	1	3				

(b) Draw an x axis from 0 to 6 and a y axis from -1 to 12.
Plot the points from the table of values onto the graph.
Join them with a straight line.
Make the line a bit longer so that it crosses the y-axis.

(c) Where does the graph of $y = 2x - 1$ cross the y-axis?

(d) Will the point (7, 13) be on the graph of $y = 2x - 1$?
How do you know?

2 **(a)** Copy and complete this table of values for $y = 2x$.

x	0	1	2	3	4
$y = 2x$	0	2			

(b) Draw an x axis from 0 to 5 and a y axis from 0 to 10.
Plot the points from the table of values and join them with a
straight line.

(c) Now make your own table of values for $y = x$.
Plot the points on the same axes as in part **(b)**.

(d) What do you notice about the two straight lines?

(e) Will the point (6, 7) be on the graph of $y = x$?
How do you know?

Finishing off

Now that you have finished this chapter you should be able to:

● plot and use positive and negative co-ordinates
● make a table of values and use it to draw a graph.

Review exercise

SU

1 Look at this grid.

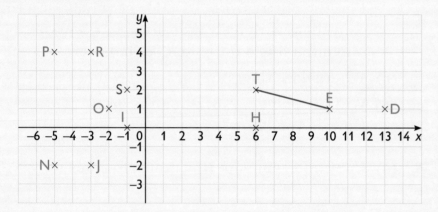

(a) Use the co-ordinates and letters of the points to solve this code.

$(-3, -2)$ $(-2, 1)$ $(-1, 0)$ $(-5, -2)$

$(6, 2)$ $(6, 0)$ $(10, 1)$

                                                        S
$(-5, 4)$ $(-2, 1)$ $(-1, 0)$ $(-5, -2)$ $(6, 2)$ $(-1, 2)$

$(-1, 0)$ $(-5, -2)$

$(-2, 1)$ $(-3, 4)$ $(13, 1)$ $(10, 1)$ $(-3, 4)$

On the grid, $(-1, 2)$ is the letter S, and this has been put in for you.

(b) Follow the instructions in the message in part **(a)**. What have you drawn?

The last line has been drawn for you.

2 **(a)** Complete this table of values for $y = 3x - 3$.

x	0	2	4	6
$3x$	0	6	12	
-3	-3	-3		
$y = 3x - 3$	-3	3		

(b) Draw a grid with the x axis from 0 to 6 and the y axis from -5 to 15.

Plot the points and join them with a straight line to make the graph of $y = 3x - 3$.

(c) Use your graph to find the value of x when y is 0.

3 On this grid, points A and B **must not move**.
Point C **can** move.

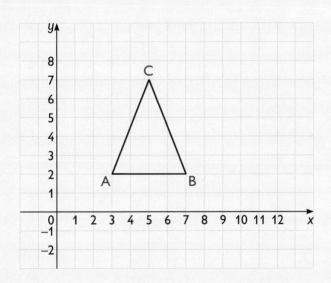

When C is at (5, 7), triangle ABC is isosceles.

(a) Point C moves to a place so that triangle ABC is still isosceles.

Write down the co-ordinates of a point that C can move to.

(b) Then C moves to a place so that triangle ABC is both isosceles **and** right-angled.

Write down the co-ordinates of a point that C can move to.

Scale drawing review

Ronnie designs rides for leisure parks.
He puts all the details onto scale drawings.

 What are scale drawings?

 Why does Ronnie need scale drawings?

Task

Here is a design for a new ride.

All the spokes of the wheel are 45° apart.

Riders sit in round pods at the end of
the spokes.

Make an accurate scale drawing of the
new ride.

Use a scale of 1 cm to 1 m.

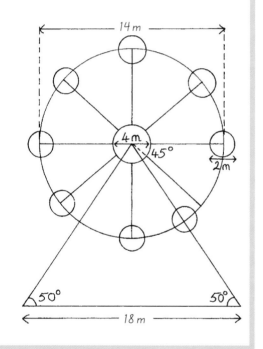

 **How tall will the ride be, including
the pods?**

At night, each pod is lit up inside.
The wheel goes round fast.

 **What shape does the path of
all the lit pods make?**

Exercise

1 Look at this scale drawing of a room.
The scale used is 1 cm to 50 cm.

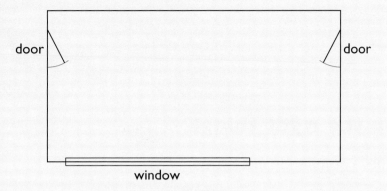

door

door

window

   (a) How wide is the real window?
   (b) How far is it in the real room from door to door?

A fireplace 2 m wide is built in the room.

   (c) How wide will the fireplace be on the scale drawing?

2 A goat is tied by a piece of rope
3.5 m long, to a small tree in the
centre of a garden lawn.

The lawn is a square, 8 m by 8 m.

   (a) Use a scale of 1 cm to 50 cm to
   make a scale drawing of the
   lawn showing the area of grass
   that the goat can eat.

Another goat is tied by a 2 m
rope to a post in one corner of the
lawn.

   (b) Show on your scale drawing the area of grass that this goat
   can eat.

   (c) Can the two goats meet?

Activity Design a ride for a leisure park.
Decide how big the real ride should be.
Construct an accurate scale drawing of the ride.

Perpendiculars and bisecting lines

Karen learns how to **bisect** a line.

❝ Do the right thing!

Follow these steps to bisect a line.

STEP 1 Open the compasses to just over half the length of the line.

STEP 2 Put the compass point on A and draw an arc.

STEP 3 Put the compass point on B and draw another arc.

STEP 4 Join the two points where the arcs cross.

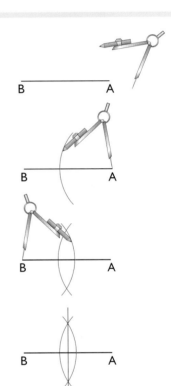

Task

1 Draw four different lines.
2 Bisect each line. Measure the lengths to check your accuracy.
3 Use a protractor to measure the angle between each line and its **bisector**.

? What does **bisect** mean?

? Describe the **symmetry** of your bisections.

? These straight lines are **perpendicular**.
What does perpendicular mean?

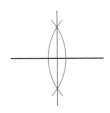

Exercise

1 Look at these pairs of lines.

(a)   (b)   (c)   (d)

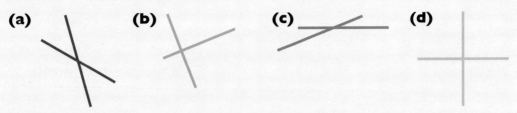

(a) Which pairs of lines are perpendicular?

(b) Which pairs of lines bisect each other?

2 **(a)** Construct an equilateral triangle with sides 10 cm long.
Carefully bisect each side of the triangle.
What do you notice?

(b) Now construct an isosceles triangle with two sides 10 cm long
and the other 6 cm long.
Bisect each side of this triangle.
What do you notice?

(c) Now construct a triangle with sides 12 cm, 9 cm and 7 cm long.
Bisect each side of this triangle.
What do you notice?

3 Look at these buildings. Which of them are perpendicular to
the ground?

Bisecting angles

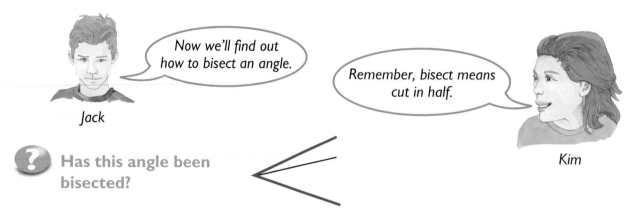

Now we'll find out how to bisect an angle.

Jack

Remember, bisect means cut in half.

Kim

? **Has this angle been bisected?**

" **Do the right thing!**

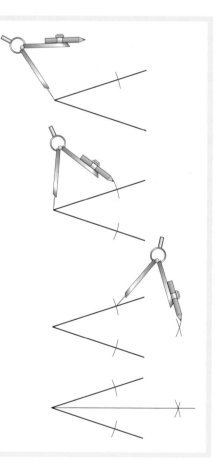

STEP 1 Draw an angle on a piece of paper.

STEP 2 Open the compasses. Put their point on the point of the angle.

STEP 3 Make arcs on each of the arms of the angle. Keep the compasses open to the same distance all the time.

STEP 4 Put the point of the compasses on one of the arcs. Make another arc between the arms of the angle.
Repeat with the other arc.

STEP 5 Join the point where the arcs cross with the point of the angle.

Task

1 Draw 4 different angles and construct their bisectors.
2 Use a protractor to check your accuracy.

? If you bisect a right angle, what size angle do you make?

Exercise

1 Look at these angles.

(a) 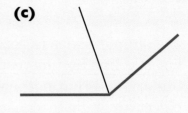   **(b)**   **(c)**

Which angles have been bisected?

2 Use a protractor to draw these angles.

(a) 60°   **(b)** 110°   **(c)** 36°   **(d)** 154°

Using a ruler and a pair of compasses, construct the bisector for each angle.
Measure each new angle to check that your construction is accurate.

Investigation

Draw an equilateral triangle accurately.
Bisect its 3 angles.
What do you notice?

Now draw an isosceles triangle and bisect its angles.
Do you notice the same thing?

What about a scalene triangle?

Activity

Draw a horizontal line 12 cm long.

Now, using only your ruler and a pair of compasses, construct this spider's web.

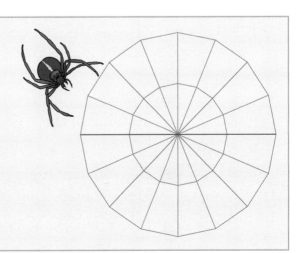

Finishing off

Now that you have finished this chapter you should be able to:

● use simple scales in scale drawing
● bisect a line by construction
● understand that perpendicular lines are at right angles to each other
● bisect an angle by construction.

Review exercise

1 Look at Pirate Pete's treasure map.

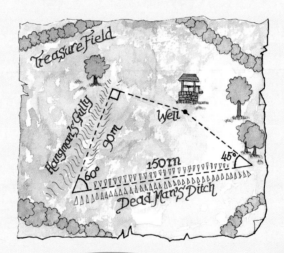

The treasure lies where the perpendicular bisectors of Hangman's Gully and Dead Man's Ditch meet.

Pete

(a) Use a ruler and compasses to construct an accurate scale drawing of the treasure field. **Do not use a protractor!** Use a scale of 1 cm to 10 m.

(b) Use constructions to find the exact position of the treasure. Mark the position of the treasure with a 'T'.

(c) How far is the treasure from the well?

2 **(a)** Make an accurate construction of this triangle.

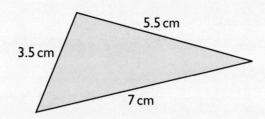

(b) Bisect each angle of the triangle.

(c) Where do the three bisectors meet?

3 Look at this regular hexagon.

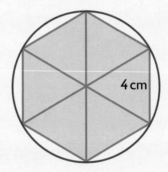

The hexagon has been drawn inside a circle.

(a) Draw a circle with a radius of 4 cm.
Use a ruler and compasses to construct the hexagon inside it.

(b) Bisect each of the angles at the centre of the hexagon.
Use the bisectors to make a 12-sided regular polygon.

Activity

Use a ruler and compasses to construct these angles.

1 135°   **2** 270°   **3** 240°   **4** 210°   **5** 15°

Averages review

Visit Brightsea

Average of 8 hours of sunshine a day throughout August.

Here are the hours of sunshine for a week last August.

7, 11, 10, 7, 7, 9, 5

? Find the mean, the median and the mode.

? Do you agree with the poster?
Which average have you used?

? What is the range for the hours of sunshine?

Task

You are going to work out the number of children per family for the students in your class.

1 Make a list of the number of people under 18 living in each home.

2 Work out the mean, the median and the mode for your data.

3 You must choose one average. Which do you choose?

4 Explain your choice.

? The average size for the whole country is 1.7 children per family.
Do your results agree with this?

? For your class, find the range of the number of children in a family.

Exercise

1 Find the means of these sets of data.

  (a) 2, 2, 3, 5, 7, 8, 9, 9, 10, 12   (b) 23, 24, 26, 29, 35

2 Find the means of these sets of data.

  (a) 4, 6, 9, 12, 12, 13, 15, 20   (b) 6, 4, 10 , 3, 9, 12, 11, 7

3 Find the modes of these sets of data.

  (a) 10, 11, 12, 12, 14, 17, 19   (b) 2, 5, 1, 2, 1, 4, 2, 3

4

I cycle an average of 10 km a day.

Kim

These are the distances Kim cycles one week.

  9.8 km, 10 km, 12 km, 9.7 km, 11 km, 9.9 km, 10 km

  (a) Find the mean, median and mode of these distances.

  (b) Is Kim correct?

5

Mum, my pocket money is below average.

Jack

These are the amounts of pocket money given to Jack's friends.

  £1, £1.50, £2.50, £2.50, £1.50, £2.00, £1.75, £2.50

Jack gets £2.00 pocket money.

  (a) Which average is he using?

  (b) Is Jack being fair to his mother?

Comparing sets of data

Ali looks at her marks in 3 subjects this year.
She works out the mean and range for each subject.

Subject	Mean mark (%)	Range
French	52	25
Geography	48	10
Art	45	12

? Which subject has the highest mean mark?

? Which subject shows the most consistent performance?

> Look at the range to answer this.

> I have to choose 1 subject to study in year 10.

Ali

? Ali chooses geography. Is this a sensible choice?

Task

Three athletes enter the long jump trial for their club.

Athlete	Length of jump (metres)
John Smith	2.9, 3.5, 2.8, 3.4, 2.6, 2.8, 2.9, 3.0, 3.2, 2.8
Brian Raj	2.7, 2.8, 3.1, 3.3, 2.9, 3.4, 2.7, 2.9, 3.1, 3.0
Zak Trent	2.7, 2.6, 3.5, 2.4, 3.6, 2.3, 2.7, 2.6, 2.4, 2.8

1 How many jumps does each athlete do?
2 Find the mean length of jump for each athlete.
3 Find the range for each athlete.
4 Which athlete has the longest jump?
5 Which athlete do you choose to represent the club?
   Give a reason for your choice.

? It is important to look at the range as well as the mean when comparing sets of data. Give a reason for this.

Exercise

1 Sam uses 2 different fertilisers on his tomatoes.
The table shows the mean and range for the number of tomatoes on his plants.

Fertiliser	Mean	Range
Growmore	21	13
Organic mix	19	5

(a) Which fertiliser gives the better average number of tomatoes?

(b) Which fertiliser gives the lower range?

(c) Sam decides to use Growmore next year. Has he made the right choice?

2 Jo is deciding where to go for her holidays.
Here are the sunshine hours at 2 resorts for a week last August.

Resort	Sunshine hours
Abercliff	6, 10, 1, 7, 11, 3, 4
Brightsea	5, 8, 4, 6, 5, 6, 8

(a) Calculate the mean sunshine hours for each resort.

(b) Find the range of sunshine hours for each resort.

(c) Jo decides to go to Brightsea. Why has she made this choice?

3 Here are the 5 best javelin throws for 3 athletes.

Athlete	Length of throw (metres)
Ben Jason	61, 82, 73, 59, 81
Chris White	72, 70, 69, 64, 75
Mel Cox	63, 59, 58, 65, 69

(a) Find the mean and range for each athlete.

(b) Chris White is chosen to represent his team.
Why is he the most reliable athlete?

Grouping data

Humza counts the letters in 100 words from his English book.
He draws a table and bar chart to show his results.

> *The table is called a* **grouped frequency table**.

> *This group shows the words with 7, 8 or 9 letters.*

Number of letters	Frequency (number of words)
1-3	31
4-6	47
7-9	14
10-12	6
13-15	2

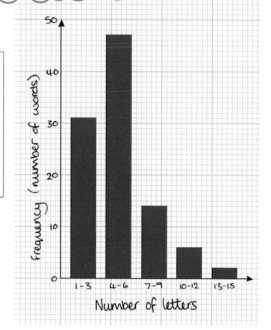

? How many words have 1, 2 or 3 letters?

? Which group in the table is the most common?

Task

Count the number of letters in 100 words from a book you are reading.
Use a copy of this table to collect your results.

Number of letters	Tally	Frequency (number of words)
1–3		
4–6		
7–9		
10–12		
13–15		
over 15		

Draw a bar chart to show your results.
What is the modal group?

Compare your results from the task with other people's.

 Do you all have the same modal group?

Exercise

1 Pete has drawn this table to show the lengths of 100 surnames.

Number of letters	Frequency
1–5	29
6–10	62
11–15	8
16–20	1

(a) How many surnames have 1–5 letters?

(b) Draw a bar chart to show Pete's results.

(c) Which is the modal group?

2 Alan asks his friends how many CDs they have.
Here are the results.

5, 12, 14, 22, 7, 9,   34, 57, 8, 49,   38, 25, 22, 41, 32,   22, 18, 14, 8, 27

(a) Using the groups 1–10, 11–20, 21–30, … make a grouped frequency table of Alan's results.

(b) Draw a bar chart to show the data.

(c) Which is the modal group?

Investigation

The stem-and-leaf diagram shows the heights of 20 students.

Stem	Leaf
12	5 5 6
13	2 3 3 4 6 6 8 8
14	4 5 8 9 9
15	1 2 2 3

Key: 12|5 = 125 cm

1 Why is this like a grouped frequency table?

2 How many students are more than 120 cm but less than 130 cm tall?

3 Which is the modal group?

4 Use the table to find the median height.

Finishing off

Now that you have finished this chapter you should be able to:

- find the mean, median and mode of a set of data
- use the mean and range to compare data sets
- interpret grouped frequency tables
- draw bar charts for grouped frequency.

Review exercise

1 Mike has 2 possible sites for his hot dog stand.
He spends a week at each site.
He records the number of hot dogs he sells each day.

Site A	56, 45, 32, 29, 49, 25, 61
Site B	12, 74, 35, 22, 69, 10, 44

(a) Find the median and the range for each site.

(b) Mike chooses site A. Do you agree with his choice?

2 There are 20 houses in Corner Close.
This is the number of letters the postman delivers to each house.

1, 3, 0, 2, 5,   7, 4, 10, 8, 1,   2, 0, 11, 15, 5,   18, 9, 10, 1, 6

(a) Copy the table and use it to organise these data.

Number of letters	Tally	Frequency
0–4		
5–9		
10–14		
15–19		

(b) Draw a bar chart to show the data.

Activity

Mercy

Girls' names are longer than boys' names.

How can we test that?

Mark

1 Collect at least 20 girls' and 20 boys' names.

Use the names of your friends and the students in your class.

2 Find the average (mean) length of the girls' names and the average (mean) length of the boys' names.

3 Find the range for the length of the girls' names and the range for the length of the boys' names.

4 Is there a difference?

5 Draw a poster to show your results.

Activity

1 Choose an English storybook and a French storybook.

You can choose another language. Perhaps German or Spanish …

2 Choose 100 words from each book.

… or perhaps a different English author.

3 Count the number of letters in these words.

4 Use a table like this to collect your results. Use a different table for each book.

Number of letters	Tally	Frequency
1–3		
4–6		
7–9		
10–12		
13–15		
over 15		

5 Draw a bar chart for each book.

6 Are there any differences in the length of words used?

Decimals review

Tim and Alan order some food at The Greasy Spoon café,

The Greasy Spoon
MENU
Pizza — £1.55
Curry — £1.71
Coke — 80p
Orange juice — 82p

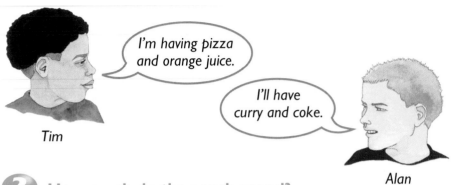

I'm having pizza and orange juice.

Tim

I'll have curry and coke.

Alan

? **How much do they each spend?**

? **How did you work it out?**

Task

1 Harry, Megan, Wayne, Samir and Michelle all eat at The Greasy Spoon.
The table shows the food that they order.
Work out how much each pays. Then copy and fill in the table.

	Burger £1.85	Chips £1.10	Muffins 75p	Tea 65p	Coke 80p	Total spent
Harry	1	1	0	1	0	
Megan	0	0	2	0	1	
Wayne	2	1	0	0	1	
Samir	0	1	0	2	2	
Michelle	1	2	2	3	0	

2 You have £3 and your friend has £5.
Choose meals for yourself and your friend.

? **When does 2 × 75 give 1.50?**

Exercise

1 How much are these snacks?

(a)

1 pasty	85p
1 orange juice	75p

(b)

1 bar of chocolate	47p
1 packet of jelly babies	£1.05

2 Copy and complete the table.

Pounds	Pence
£1.20	120
	153
	40
£0.77	
	4

3 Copy the table and write the questions, **(a)** to **(j)**, in the correct columns.

0.2	2	20	200
		a	

(a) 2×10 **(b)** 0.2×10 **(c)** 0.2×100 **(d)** 20×10

(e) 0.02×10 **(f)** $20 \div 100$ **(g)** $200 \div 10$ **(h)** 0.002×100

(i) $200 \div 100$ **(j)** $2 \div 10$

4 In each of these magic squares, the numbers in each row, column and diagonal add up to 3.
Copy the squares and find the missing numbers.

(a)

0.8		
1.8	0	

(b)

		1.6
	1	
		0.6

Activity What are the metric units for length?
Write them in metres using decimals or powers of 10.
Arrange them in order of size.

Ordering decimals

$$0.003 \quad 3\% \quad \frac{3}{10}$$

Humza

Which of these numbers is biggest?

Make them all decimals. Then you can compare them.

John

? **Compare numbers by writing them as decimals.**

Task

Make a pack of cards. Write these numbers on them.

0.1	0.01	0.02	0.2	1	0.21
0.12	2	0.22	1.2	1.1	1.01
$\frac{33}{100}$	$\frac{11}{100}$	$\frac{1}{2}$	$\frac{3}{10}$	$1\frac{1}{2}$	$1\frac{3}{100}$
$\frac{1}{20}$	$\frac{7}{10}$	$1\frac{7}{10}$	$1\frac{3}{10}$	$\frac{1}{4}$	$\frac{7}{100}$

Now play the game **More than** with a friend.

● Share the cards equally. You can look at them.
● Place one of your cards on the table.
● Your friend puts down another card.
● The person with the higher card wins both cards, and keeps them.
● Now it is your friend's turn to start.
● The game ends when there are no more cards.
● The winner is the player with most cards.

? **What are the numbers A, B, C?**

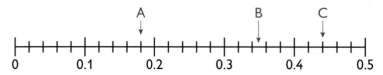

Exercise

1 Write down the readings A to D on these scales.

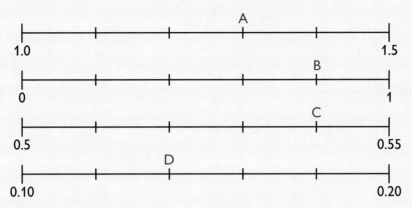

2 How many small squares are there on this grid?

Outline the grid on squared paper.

Colour 0.3 of the grid red.
Colour 0.03 of the grid blue.
Colour 0.26 of the grid yellow.
Colour 0.4 of the grid green.

How many squares are still white?
What decimal of the grid is still white?

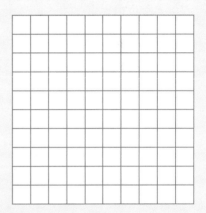

3 Arrange the numbers in order of size, smallest first.

(a) 0.7, 7, 70, 0.71, 0.07
(b) 36, 0.36, 3.6, 0.036, 0.63
(c) 45, 0.45, 0.54, 0.04, 0.005
(d) 1.11, 0.13, 1.3, 1.01, 0.31
(e) $\frac{4}{10}$, 0.04, 0.41, $\frac{14}{10}$, $\frac{104}{100}$

4 Copy these and fill in each space with any number between the two either side of it.

(a) 1.1 ——— _____ ——— 1.2 ——— _____ ——— 12

(b) 0.03 ——— _____ ——— 0.04 ——— _____ ——— 0.06

(c) 0.7 ——— _____ ——— 0.75 ——— _____ ——— 0.8

(d) 1.01 ——— _____ ——— 1.02 ——— _____ ——— 1.1

Multiplying and dividing decimals

Karl and Lucy visit the Avonford Theme Park.
They go all the way round in the train.

 How far do they ride?

 How far do they ride if they go round 3 times? 5 times?

The train ride costs £2 for each kilometre.

 How much does each part of the journey cost?

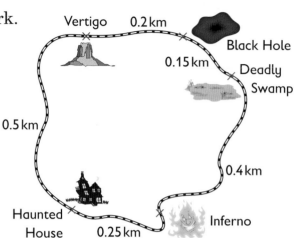

 Task

Copy the table.
Use the map to fill in the missing distances and costs.

Ride	Distance for 1 ride	Distance for 5 rides	Cost for 1 ride	Cost for 5 rides
Vertigo to Black Hole	0.2 km	5 × 0.2 = 1.0 km		
Haunted House to Black Hole	0.5 + 0.2 = 0.7 km		2 × 0.7 = £1.40	5 × £1.40 =
Inferno to Vertigo				
Deadly Swamp to Inferno				
Haunted House to Deadly Swamp				

Kim and Mark ride round the park in the train.
Their journey is 9 km.

 How many times round the park do they ride?

Exercise

1. Multiply these numbers by 2. **(a)** 0.35 **(b)** 4.5 **(c)** 2.2

2. Multiply these numbers by 5. **(a)** 0.7 **(b)** 3.1 **(c)** 1.25

3. Copy these multiplication squares. Fill in the missing numbers.

×	0.2	0.5
4		
7		

×	1.3	2.7
6		
10		

4. Work out these multiplications.
   (a) $0.7 \times 5 \times 3$ **(b)** $1.5 \times 3 \times 6$ **(c)** $24.6 \times 2 \times 5$

5. Work out these divisions.
   (a) $0.8 \div 4$ **(b)** $25.5 \div 5$ **(c)** $18.48 \div 3$

6. **(a)** Find the entry cost for Mr and Mrs Jones and their children John (12 years) and Joanna (8 years).

   (b) Find the entry cost for Sue Smith and her daughter Sally (3 years).

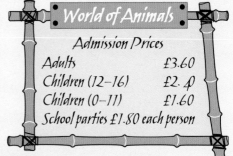

World of Animals

Admission Prices

Adults	£3.60
Children (12–16)	£2.40
Children (0–11)	£1.60

School parties £1.80 each person

   (c) Mr and Mrs Thomas pay £5.60 for their three children. How old are their children?

   (d) Some students from class 9G go to World of Animals. They pay £19.80. How many students go?

Activity

Plan an animal park.
Copy and use the grid.

Draw in the animal pens.
Draw the paths round the park.
Write down the distances.
Use decimals of 1 km.

How far is it to go all the way round?

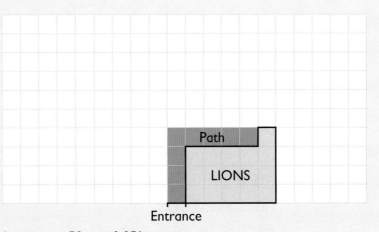

1 square = 50 m = 0.05 km

Finishing off

Now that you have finished this chapter you should be able to:

- multiply and divide by 10 and 100
- add and subtract decimals
- place decimals in order
- multiply and divide decimals.

Review exercise

1 Meena is buying some toy animals for her baby brother.

£4.95

£6.65

£4.25

£2.35

Find the cost of these.

(a) an elephant and a giraffe

(b) a giraffe and a monkey

(c) a monkey and a lion

(d) 2 giraffes

(e) 2 monkeys

(f) 2 lions and an elephant

2 Copy and complete these.
The answer is always 10 or 100.

(a) $2.1 \times \boxed{} = 21$ (b) $2.1 \div \boxed{} = 0.021$

(c) $21 \div \boxed{} = 2.1$ (d) $21 \times \boxed{} = 2100$

(e) $0.021 \times \boxed{} = 2.1$ (f) $0.21 \div \boxed{} = 0.021$

(g) $0.021 \times \boxed{} = 0.21$ (h) $2.1 \times \boxed{} = 210$

3 Write these numbers in order of size, starting with the smallest.

(a) 3.5   35   5.3   0.003   0.05   0.0035   0.35

(b) 0.71   7.1   0.071   0.17   0.1   17   0.7

4 Fill in the tables.

×	0.2	1.5
3		
8		

×	0.15	2.5
4		
7		

5 Calculate these.

(a) 40×10 (b) $4 \div 10$ (c) $400 \div 10$ (d) 0.4×10

(e) $0.4 \div 10$ (f) $40 \div 100$ (g) 0.4×100 (h) 0.04×10

6 Mercy and Jack do a sponsored walk for charity.
Each lap is 1.25 km.

Copy the table.
Fill in the missing numbers.

Walker	Number of laps	Distance walked	Amount sponsored per km	Amount raised
Mercy	10		£2.00	
Jack	12		£4.50	

Expressions

Sophie, Jo and Pete buy some computer games.

Jo

Sophie

Pete

How many games are you getting?

I am buying 3 more games than you, Jo.

I am buying twice as many games as Jo.

Pete writes this.

> Jo   Sophie   Me
> g $g + 3$ $2g$
> Altogether we bought $g + g + 3 + 2g$ games

*These are **expressions**.*

? **What does *g* stand for? What does 2g mean?**

Pete simplifies his expression.

> $g + g + 3 + 2g = 4g + 3$

? **Pete buys 2 games. How many games do they buy altogether?**

Task

I Here are some **Algebra snap** cards. Match them together.

$3a + a$	$2 \times 2a$	$5a + 3 - a - 3$	$2a + 3a + 2 + 1$
$5a + 3$	$2a + 2a$	$a + a + a + a$	$2a + 5 + 3a - 2$

2 Play a game of **Algebra snap** with a partner.

Look how Pete simplifies $3a + 2b - a + 4b + 2a$.

> group together like terms : $3a + 2b - a + 4b + 2a$
> $3a - a + 2a + 2b + 4b$
> $4a + 6b$

? **Can Pete simplify this any further? What does 'like terms' mean?**

? **How should you write (a)** $5a - 4a$ **(b)** $3b - 2b - b$?

Exercise

1 Simplify these expressions.

(a) $3a + 2a + a$ (b) $5b - 3b$ (c) $3c + 4c - 5c$

(d) $5d + 4d + 3d$ (e) $4e + 5e - 8e$ (f) $5f - 4f - f$

2 Simplify these expressions.

(a) $3a + 4a + 2b + 4b$ (b) $6a + 2b - 4a + 3b$

(c) $7c + 3 - 4c + 2$ (d) $6d + 6 - 5d - 5$

(e) $4d + 3e - 3d - 2e$ (f) $4e + 3f - 2f - 3e - e$

SU

3 Copy and complete these algebra walls.
Each brick is found by adding together the expressions in the two bricks underneath it.
Find the missing expressions.

(a)
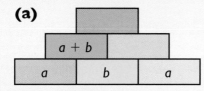

$a + b$	

a	b	a

(b)
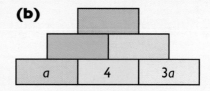

a	4	$3a$

(c)
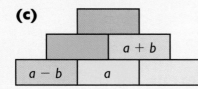

	$a + b$

$a - b$	a	

(d)
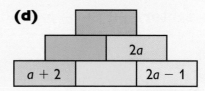

	$2a$

$a + 2$		$2a - 1$

4 Ali has some toffees.

(a) Write down expressions for the
number of sweets each person has.
Use t for the number of toffees Ali has.

Ali

*I have 4
more toffees
than Ali.*

*I have 2 less
toffees than Ali.*

Alan

Samir

*I have twice as
many toffees as Ali.*

Christina

(b) How many toffees do they have altogether?

Brackets

Megan writes down an expression for the area of this rectangle.

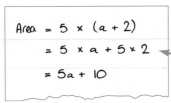

	a	2
5	$5 \times a$	5×2

Area = 5 × (a + 2)
    = 5 × a + 5 × 2
    = 5a + 10

Megan has **expanded** the brackets.

? **How can you check that**
$5 \times (a + 2) = 5a + 10$?

The perimeter of my rectangle is $2(a + 7)$

? **Is Megan right?**

Megan

Another rectangle has a perimeter of $4a + 8$.

? **What can the length and width of this rectangle be?**

Megan writes:

$$4a + 8 = 4(a + 2)$$

You don't need the × sign.

Megan has **factorised** the expression **fully**.

Task

These rectangles are **all different**, but they all have the same area of $12a + 24$.

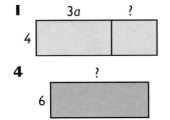

1 3a   ?
   4

2 ?a   ?
   2

3 a + 2
   ?

4   ?
   6

5 4(a + 2)
   ?

6   ?
   ?

(a) Find the missing lengths.   **(b)** Find the perimeter of each rectangle.
(c) Write your answers to **(b)** using brackets.

This is called **factorising**.

(d) What is the perimeter of each rectangle when $a = 3$?

? **How should you write these?**
   (a) $5 \times 3 \times n$ **(b)** $4 \times 2n$ **(c)** $a \times b$ **(d)** $a \times a$

? Expand $4(2a - 3)$.
   Factorise $8a + 4$ fully.

Exercise

1 Find the value of the following.

(a) $4(n + 3)$ when (i) $n = 2$ (ii) $n = 3$

(b) $3(x - 4)$ when (i) $x = 5$ (ii) $x = 6$

(c) $2(a + b)$ when (i) $a = 2, b = 3$ (ii) $a = 3, b = 4$

(d) $3(2c - 3)$ when (i) $c = 4$ (ii) $c = 2$

(e) $6(2d - 3e)$ when (i) $d = 2, e = 1$ (ii) $d = 3, e = 2$

2 Find expressions for the areas of these rectangles.

(a)

	a	4
2		

(b)

	$3b$	6
3		

(c)

	b	c
a		

3 Expand these brackets.

(a) $2(a + 3)$ (b) $3(b + 5)$ (c) $8(c - 2)$

(d) $5(d + e)$ (e) $4(2e + 3)$ (f) $6(2f - 1)$

4 Factorise the following.

(a) $2a + 4$ (b) $3b + 9$ (c) $7c + 7$

(d) $3d - 3e$ (e) $5e - 10$ (f) $10f - 5$

5 (a) Find as many ways as you can to factorise these.

(i) $6a + 12$ (ii) $10b - 20$ (iii) $36c + 24$

(b) Factorise each expression fully.

6 Here are some **Algebra snap** cards.
Match them together.

$4(9n + 6)$

$12(3n + 2)$

$10n + 15$

$2(18n + 12)$

$5(2n + 3)$

$6(3n - 1)$

$18n - 12$

$6(3n - 2)$

$36n + 24$

$18n - 6$

$3(6n - 2)$

$3(6n - 4)$

Finishing off

Now that you have finished this chapter you should:

- know the meaning of the words **expression**, **simplify**, **like** and **unlike terms**, **factorise** and **expand**
- be able to
  - simplify an expression
  - factorise an expression
  - expand brackets.

Review exercise

1 Simplify these expressions.

    (a) $a + a + a + a$ **(b)** $b + 2b + 3b - 4b$

    (c) $3c + 4 - 2c - 3$ **(d)** $4d + 4e - 3d - e - 3e$

2 Expand the following.

    (a) $2(a + 3)$ **(b)** $4(a + b)$ **(c)** $3(2c - 3)$

3 Factorise these fully.

    (a) $6a + 6b$ **(b)** $5b + 10$ **(c)** $8c - 12$

4 Find the values of the following.

    (a) $3(a - 2)$ when   **(i)** $a = 3$ **(ii)** $a = 5$

    (b) $5(2b + 1)$ when   **(i)** $b = 1$ **(ii)** $b = 2$

    (c) $4(2c - d)$ when   **(i)** $c = 2, d = 3$ **(ii)** $c = 3, d = 6$

5 **(a)** Write down expressions for

    (i) the perimeter of this square

    (ii) the area of the square.

(b) This rectangle has a perimeter of $6a + 10$.
Write down an expression for

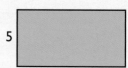

    (i) the length of the rectangle

    (ii) the area of the rectangle.

6 Kim has a bag with $8n + 12$ sweets.
She gives $3n + 7$ sweets to Andy.

(a) Write down an expression for the number of sweets Kim has left.

(b) How many sweets does each person have when $n = 5$?
How many more sweets does Kim have than Andy?

(c) Kim now shares the $8n + 12$ sweets equally between them.
Write down an expression for the number of sweets Andy has.

7 This is a magic square.

$a - b$	$a + b - c$	$a + c$
$a + b + c$	a	$a - b - c$
$a - c$	$a - b + c$	$a + b$

(a) Add together the expressions in each row.

(b) Add together the expressions in each column.

(c) Add together the expressions in each diagonal.

(d) What do you notice?

(e) Make the magic square for $a = 5$, $b = 1$ and $c = 3$.

(f) Choose some other numbers for a, b and c. Make your own magic square.

Investigation

Another way of writing $n \div n$ is $\dfrac{n}{n}$.

1 Find the values of **(a)** $\dfrac{n}{n}$ **(b)** $\dfrac{2n}{n}$

when **(i)** $n = 2$ **(ii)** $n = 3$ **(iii)** $n = 4$

2 What do **(a)** $\dfrac{n}{n}$ **(b)** $\dfrac{2n}{n}$ always equal?

3 How should you write these?

(a) $\dfrac{4n}{n}$ **(b)** $\dfrac{10n}{n}$ **(c)** $\dfrac{100n}{n}$

Rectangular shapes review

I remember all about perimeter and area.

Mercy

Perimeter is the distance all the way round a shape

Area is an amount of flat surface

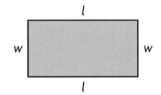

 How do you find the perimeter of a shape?

 What formula do you use for the area of a rectangle?

Task

Ellie is giving her family three pictures.

(a) 15 cm, 10 cm

(b) 8 cm, 12 cm

(c) 15 cm, 15 cm

She makes the frames herself.
The wood for the frames comes in 1 m lengths costing £2.25 each.
Ellie cuts the glass herself. It costs 5p per cm².

1 How much wood does Ellie need for each frame?

2 How much wood does she buy altogether? What does it cost?

3 What area of glass does she need for each photograph?

4 How much does the glass cost altogether?

5 How much do the three frames cost Ellie altogether?

The area of another piece of glass is 120 cm². The glass is 10 cm wide.

 How long is it? What is its perimeter?

Exercise

1 **(a)** Measure the sides of this shape.

(b) Work out its perimeter.

(c) Work out its area.

2 A rectangle has a perimeter of 18 cm, and length of 5 cm.

(a) What is the width of the rectangle?

(b) What is the area of the rectangle?

3 A square has an area of 36 cm².

(a) What is the length of one side of the square?

(b) What is its perimeter?

4 Amit and Hamid are groundsmen at the Avonford Rugby Club. Amit mows the grass and Hamid marks out the pitch.

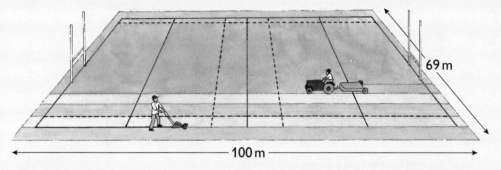

69 m

100 m

(a) Who looks after the perimeter of the pitch and who looks after the area?

(b) What is the perimeter of the pitch?

(c) What is the area of the pitch?

Activity Measure the length and width of your school sports hall.

Work out the perimeter of the hall.

Work out the area of the hall.

Make the same measurements and calculations for your classroom.

Area of a triangle

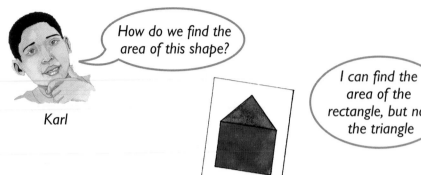

How do we find the area of this shape?

Karl

I can find the area of the rectangle, but not the triangle

Tim

? How do you find the total area of a shape like this?

? What do you need to know first?

Task

On centimetre squared paper, draw all the possible rectangles with area 12 cm². On each rectangle, draw a diagonal.

Remember, a diagonal goes from one corner to the opposite corner.

Cut out each rectangle.
Cut along the diagonal of each rectangle.

? What shapes have you made?

For each rectangle, fit one triangle on top of the other triangle.

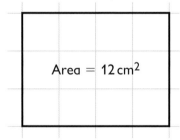

Area = 12 cm²

? What do you notice?

What is the area of your triangles?

Test your idea by counting squares in each triangle to find its area.

Sometimes, you will put two part-squares together to make a whole one.

? What have you found out about the area of a triangle?

The formula for the area of a rectangle is length × width.

? What is the formula for the area of a triangle?

Exercise

1 Find the areas of these triangles by counting squares.

(a) 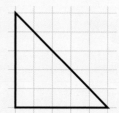 **(b)**  **(c)**

2 **(a)** Calculate the area of these rectangles.

(i)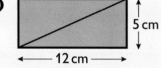
5 cm
←— 12 cm —→

(ii)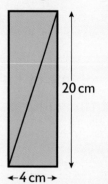
20 cm
←4 cm→

(iii)
8 cm
←8 cm→

(b) Use your answers to part **(a)** to find the areas of the triangles.

3 Calculate the areas of these triangles.

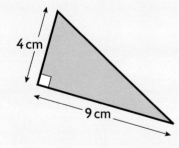
4 cm
9 cm

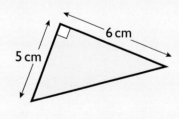
6 cm
5 cm

Investigation

The formula for the area of a right-angled triangle is 'half the base times the height'.

Humza

Is Humza's formula right?

Does it work for other sorts of triangles?

Use centimetre squared paper to test the formula.

Volume of a cuboid

Lil is an artist.
She makes a sculpture from marble.

The hole goes right through the sculpture.

? **What shape is the sculpture?**

? **What shape is the hole through the middle?**

? **How do you work out the volume of marble in the sculpture?**

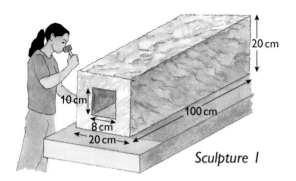

Sculpture 1

Remember, volume of a cuboid is length × width × height.

Task

(a) Work out the volume of Lil's first sculpture.

(b) Now work out the volumes of her three other sculptures.

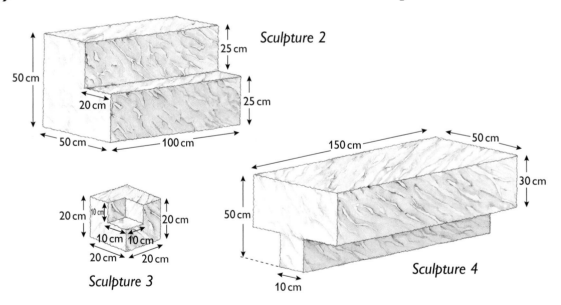

Sculpture 2

Sculpture 3

Sculpture 4

(c) How much marble is there in all the sculptures together?

? **How do you work out the volume of these sculptures?**

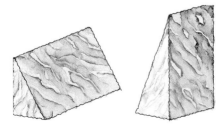

Exercise

1 Calculate the volume of these cuboids.

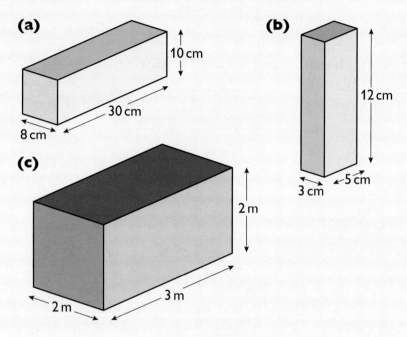

(a)
10 cm
30 cm
8 cm

(b)
12 cm
3 cm
5 cm

(c)
2 m
2 m
3 m

2 Calculate the volume of these shapes.

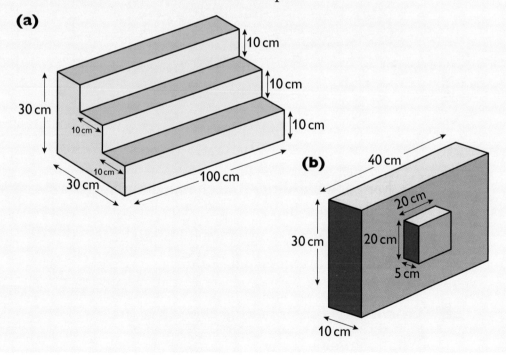

(a)
10 cm
10 cm
10 cm
30 cm
10 cm
10 cm
30 cm
100 cm

(b)
40 cm
20 cm
30 cm
20 cm
5 cm
10 cm

Finishing off

Now that you have finished this chapter you should be able to find:

- the area and perimeter of a shape made from rectangles
- the area of a triangle
- the volume of a shape made from cuboids.

Review exercise

1 Look at the plans of these school buildings.

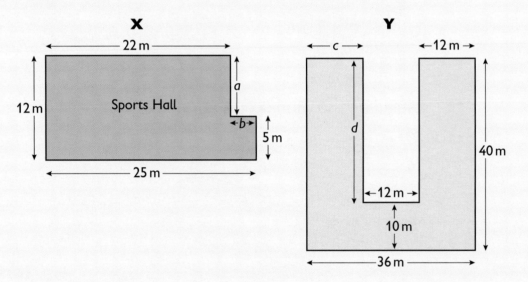

(a) For each building, find the missing lengths a and b in **X**, and c and d in **Y**.

(b) Find the perimeter of each building.

(c) Find the area of each building.

2 Look at this tin for baking cakes.

What volume of cake mixture does the tin hold when it is half full?

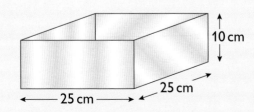

3 Find the area of each of these triangles.

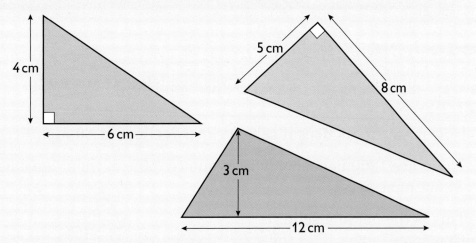

4 Pete is building a toy castle. This is his design for the front wall of the castle.

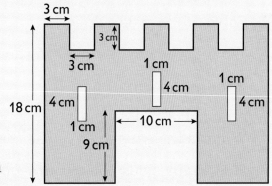

(a) Work out the area of wood used to make this wall.

(b) Pete cuts the wall out from a sheet of wood 30 cm long and 25 cm wide. How much wood is wasted?

5 This garden fountain is made from solid blocks of concrete.

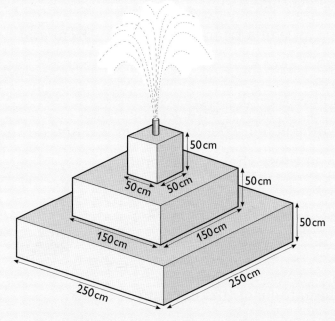

Work out the total volume of concrete needed to build the fountain.

Coded message

For each question, match your answer to a letter in the **code**, then work out the **message**.

1 How many hours does it take a car travelling at 60 mph to cover 180 miles?

2 There are 1250 households in Avonford. 60% of them have pets. How many do not have pets?

3 This is the net of a solid.
How many edges does the solid have?

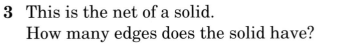

4 Solve $5f - 8 = 32$

5 What is the next number in the sequence 3, 7, 11,   ?

6 What is 11 more than -3?

7 A model of a glider has a wing span of 30 cm. The scale is 1 cm : 1 m. What is the wing span of the real aircraft in metres?

8 How many sides has a pentagon?

9 These are Halley's batting scores in cricket last season.

12, 29, 0, 53, 38, 11, 31, 25, 19, 32

What is his average?

10 What is the area of a triangle with base 18 cm and height 10 cm?

11 Work out $(2 + 4) \times 4$

12 What is $\frac{2}{3}$ of 36?

13 Find the value of $5m$, add $2n$, when $m = 8$ and $n = 5$.

14 How many of these shapes are similar?

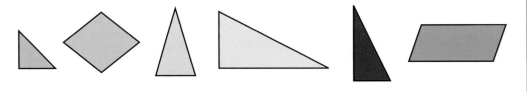

15 What is the volume of this hot tub?

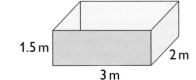

1.5 m   2 m   3 m

16 What is the perimeter of a field 25 m by 20 m?

17 Round 19.49 to nearest whole number.

18 How many lines of symmetry does this shape have?

19 Find the highest number of points that lie on a straight line.
(0, 0), (1, 2), (2, 2), (4, 3), (5, 5)

20 The new extension to the Avonford Rowing Club costs £232 848.21
What is this to the nearest £1000.

21 What is 25% of 60?

22 How many US dollars does Sheila get for £45?

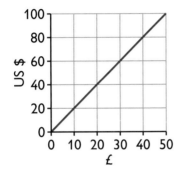

23 A survey of favourite James Bond films gives these results.
How many people were interviewed?

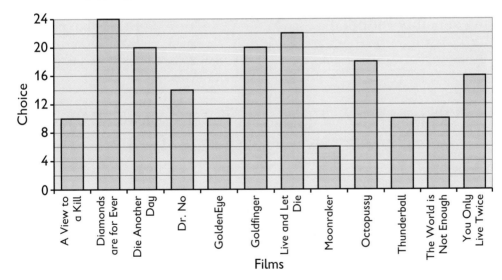

24 A bag holding 1000 coins breaks. How many coins do you expect to land heads?

25 Work out 72 ÷ 24.

Code

Answer	8	180	500	90	19	24	30	15	233 000	9	50	3	25	5
Letter	E	G	H	I	K	L	M	N	O	R	S	T	W	Y

Rounding

The Avonford Star

New Cricket Stadium to cost £2 541 161.39

? Give this cost
   (a) to the nearest £1   **(b)** to the nearest £100
   (c) to the nearest £1000   **(d)** to the nearest £1 000 000.

? Which is the most useful figure?

Task

Here is part of the article.

1 Copy and fill in the table.

2 Work out how much more
   money is needed. Give the
   answer as a rounded number.

3 Rewrite these parts of the
   article using sensibly rounded
   figures.

(a) Ian Starr, manager of Avonford Cricket Club, explained that his cost was made up of £547 778.45 for raw materials, £365 112.17 for new seating and £1 628 270.77 for labour.

(b) Mr T O'Hara, the club chairman, said that so far they only have £1 078 469.62 to pay for the work.

Item	Cost (£)	Rounded to nearest £1	Rounded to nearest £10	Rounded to nearest £100	Rounded to nearest £1000
Raw materials	547 778.45		547 780		
Seating					
Labour					

? A cricket season ticket will cost £155.

That's £160 to the nearest £10.

That's £150 to the nearest £10.

Who is right?   *Meena*   *Jack*

Exercise

1 Round these to the nearest whole number.

(a) 14.7   (b) 129.63   (c) 20.5   (d) 11.21   (e) 3021.6

2 Round these to the nearest 10.

(a) 288   (b) 53   (c) 1056   (d) 25   (e) 48993

3 Round these to the nearest 100.

(a) 96   (b) 166   (c) 231   (d) 4518   (e) 61380

4 Are these true or false?

(a) 76.3 is about 76   (b) 457.8 is about 48

(c) 141.5 is about 141   (d) 9607 is about 9600

(e) 47 132 is about 4713   (f) 191 is about 200

5 Rewrite these statements using sensibly rounded figures.

(a)
The batting average of a top Avonford batsman is 41.64.

(b)
The average gate at Avonford Town's football league matches is 2 788.37

(c)
In a typical year, Avonford Council spend £89 187 on games fields.

(d)
In a typical year, Avonford Cricket Club teams score 15 893 runs.

Activity   Look in some magazines.

Find adverts with prices. Cut them out and make them into a poster.

Show how each price could be rounded.

Decimal places

How many goals per match do you score?

Too many decimal places are confusing. You should say 0.57.

Harry

I've scored 4 goals in 7 matches. My average is 0.571 428 571 4.

Humza

 Which answer is right?

Which answer is better?

Task

These are results from the Premiership table, 1997–2003.

Year	Winning team	Goals		Points	Average goals per match		Average points per match
		F	**A**		**F**	**A**	
1997–8	Arsenal	68	33	78			
1998–9	Manchester United	80	37	79			
1999–00	Manchester United	97	45	91			
2000–1	Manchester United	79	31	80			
2001–2	Arsenal	79	36	87			
2002–3	Manchester United	74	34	83			
2003–4	Arsenal	73	26	90			

 1 Copy the table and add the missing numbers. There are 38 matches in the Premiership season. Give your answers to 2 decimal places.

2 Find the average number of goals scored for and against the winning team in each of the seven seasons. Give your answers to 1 decimal place.

What happens when you round 4.993 to
(a) 2 decimal places (b) 1 decimal place. (c) the nearest whole number?

Exercise

1 Copy this table and colour the numbers
 • with 1 decimal place in red
 • with 2 decimal places in blue
 • with 3 decimal places in yellow.

1.7	0.111	5.5	23.23
2.006	0.4	0.04	236.809
23.8	115.66	10.1	700.09
0.40	2.021	1.99	468.9

2 **(i)** Write these numbers to 1 decimal place.
 (a) 0.333 **(b)** 1.333 **(c)** 5.333 **(d)** 5.033 **(e)** 5.066
 (f) 0.066 **(g)** 10.066 **(h)** 5.366 **(i)** 5.336 **(j)** 5.666

(ii) Then write each to 2 decimal places.

3 Some fractions give never-ending decimals. Use a calculator to give the first 7 decimal places for the following.

 (a) $\frac{1}{9}$ **(b)** $\frac{2}{7}$ **(c)** $\frac{1}{6}$ **(d)** $\frac{5}{6}$

Round your answers to 2 decimal places.

> Example
> $\frac{1}{7} = 1 \div 7$
> $= 0.14257142\ldots$
> $= 0.14$ (2 decimal places)

4 For each case, think of a number and write it down.
 (a) more than 10, with 2 decimal places
 (b) between 6 and 7, with 1 decimal place
 (c) more than 100, with 1 decimal place
 (d) between 10 and 20, with 3 decimal places

Activity Investigate how to format cells on a spreadsheet to a given number of decimal places.

	A	B	C	D	E
1		1 d.p.	2 d.p.	3 d.p.	4 d.p.
2	1.316779	1.3	1.32	1.317	1.3168
3	15.90557	15.9	15.91	15.906	15.9056
4	230.8964	230.9	230.90	230.896	230.8964
5	4509.556	4509.6	4509.56	4509.556	4509.5560

Estimating and checking

Kim

How much for 3 magazines?

About 3 × £2 = £6

John

Look at what John says.

? What is 3 × £2? What is 3 × £1.85?
Which is easier to work out?

? Which is the exact answer and which is an estimate?

Task

1 Use rounding to give a rough estimate for these costs.

2 Use your answers to question **1** to estimate the costs of each of these purchases.
  (a) 2 tubes of sweets **(b)** 4 T-shirts
  (c) 5 CDs **(d)** 7 cans of drink

3 Shahab has £30. He wants to buy
  • a T shirt • a CD
  • 5 cans of drink • 3 tubes of sweets.
  Does he have enough money?
  Check your answer with a calculator.

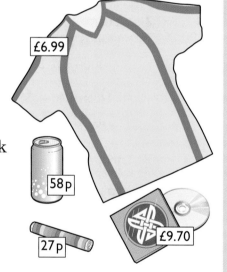

£6.99

58p

27p

£9.70

? What sort of rounding is each person doing?

Jo

The CD player is about £173

Ali

I think it is £170

£172.80

I get £200

Michelle

Exercise

1 Jan and her friends want to buy
3 bars of chocolate and 4 drinks.
They have £5. Use estimates to work
out if they have enough money.

96p 68p

2 Sophie does 7.86 × 12.48 on her calculator. She gets 20.34.
She checks by working out 8 × 12. Work this out.
What does this tell Sophie?

su

3 Lucy does these questions on her calculator.
Fill in a copy of the table to check her answers.

Question	Lucy's answer	Check	Checking answer	✓ or ✗
33 × 7	2310	30 × 7	210	
1.8 × 4.8	8.64			
6.3 × 6.3	12.96			
7.69 × 4.28	11.97			
97 × 46	4462			
882 ÷ 9.1	9.69			

4 Ages are rounded to the nearest year.

Charlie,
4 years 10 months

Rover,
7 years 2 months

Brandy,
10 years 6 months

Estimate how old each dog is in
human years.

One dog year is
7 human years.

Pete

Activity Measure your bedroom. Estimate the area of the walls.
Find out how much paint is in a tin. What area does it cover?
How many tins of paint would you need to paint your walls?

Finishing off

Now that you have finished this chapter you should be able to:
• round numbers to the nearest 1, 10, 100
• use decimal places in rounding
• estimate and check answers using rounding.

Review exercise

1 The numbers below have been rounded.
Copy the table and write each number in the correct box.

Nearest 1	To 1 decimal place	Nearest 10	To 2 decimal places

(a) 46.2   **(b)** 460   **(c)** 46.27

(d) 466   **(e)** 46.02   **(f)** 46.0

(g) 400   **(h)** 46.7   **(i)** 46

2 Use rounding to estimate the total cost of these items.

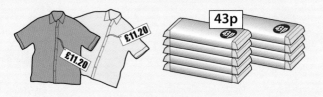

3 Copy the table. Fill in the missing numbers.

Number	Rounded to nearest 1	Rounded to nearest 10	Rounded to nearest 100	Rounded to 1 decimal place	Rounded to 2 decimal places
110.178					
84.9222					
4506.467					

SU

4 Christina does some sums on her calculator.
Copy and fill in the table to check her answers.

Sum	Calculator answer	Check	Checking answer	✓ or ✗
4.3 × 112	481.6			
99 × 42.7	4227.3			
192 ÷ 11.6	16.55			
4341 ÷ 22	19.73			

5 Use estimation to check these calculations.

(a) 57 × 1.8 = 102.6

(b) 311 ÷ 2.7 = 11.52

(c) 7.9 × 14.8 = 1169.2

(d) 4332 ÷ 37 = 117.08

6 Karl and Tim each buy a bicycle, but they pay in different ways.

Karl pays £179.99.
Tim pays £8.09 for 31 weeks.

Answer this as quickly as you can.
Who pays more?
How did you work out the answer?

20 Real-life graphs

Line graphs

Verity is 10 years old. Look at this graph of her height against age.

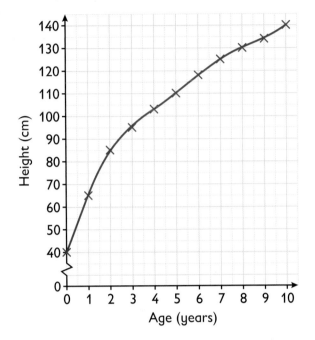

? What are the scales on the two axes?

? How tall was Verity on her 1st birthday? On her 4th birthday?

? How old was Verity when she was 130 cm high?

Task

1 Make a table for Verity's height by reading from the graph.

2 Draw a larger graph of Verity's height.
  Make the height scale go from 0 to 200.

On the day she was born, her father planted a monkey puzzle tree.

3 This table gives the height of the monkey puzzle tree each year.
  Add a graph of these heights to Verity's.

Year	0	1	2	3	4	5	6	7	8	9	10
Height	4	10	15	20	26	35	45	70	125	155	190

4 How tall was the tree when it was 5 years 6 months old?

5 When were the tree and Verity the same height?

6 Who was growing faster between years 5 and 6?

? What will happen to Verity's height in 10 years? To the tree's height?

? Can you use your graph to find out the tree's height when it is 25 years old?

Exercise

Maya and Chaya go on holiday to India.

1 They compare the temperatures in Darjeeling and Avonford over one week.

Temperature (°C)							
	Mon	Tue	Wed	Thur	Fri	Sat	Sun
Darjeeling	10	9	6	5	5	5	9
Avonford	8	9	10	10	12	8	7

(a) Draw a graph showing the temperatures in the two places.

(b) Name the warmer place on
  (i) Monday **(ii)** Wednesday **(iii)** Friday **(iv)** Sunday

(c) What place has the highest temperature?

(d) Which day is the warmest?

(e) When do the two places have the same temperature?

2 At the time, the exchange rate is £1 = 60 rupees.

(a) Draw a conversion graph like this one. Use a whole sheet of graph paper.

(b) Convert Rs4500 into pounds.

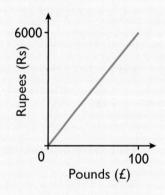

3 Maya and Chaya buy some jewellery.

(a) Maya's bangles cost Rs5500. How much did they cost in pounds?

(b) Chaya works out that her necklace is £80. How much was it in rupees?

(c) They each buy earrings. Maya's cost £15. Chaya's cost Rs750. Whose were the more expensive?

Travel graphs

Look at this **travel graph** showing the height of a hot air balloon.

(a) How high does the balloon go?

(b) For how long is the balloon at a height of 2500 m?

(c) How long does the balloon take to come down?

(d) When is the balloon at a height of 2000 m?

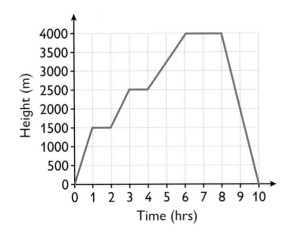

Task

1 John and Megan draw a travel graph of their walk to school. School starts at 9:00 am.

(a) When do they leave home?

(b) How long does it take them to get to school?

(c) How far away is their school?

(d) When do they have a stop?

(e) Are they late for school?

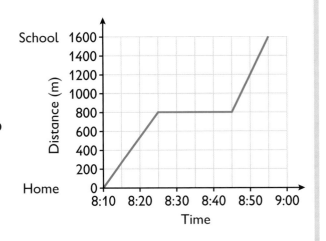

2 Work with a friend.

(a) Describe your journey to school to a friend.

(b) Draw a travel graph of your journey.

(c) Show your start and finish times.

(d) Show the distances.

Look at John and Megan's graph.

Which part shows them walking fastest?

Exercise

1 Eileen and Deep sail across the Atlantic Ocean.
This is a travel graph of their journey.

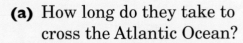
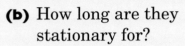
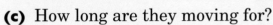
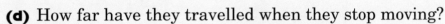

   (a) How long do they take to cross the Atlantic Ocean?

   (b) How long are they stationary for?

   (c) How long are they moving for?

   (d) How far have they travelled when they stop moving?

   (e) How wide is the Atlantic Ocean where they cross it?

2 The table shows Tom's journey to work by car.

Time	8:00	8:10	8:20	8:25	8:30	8:40
Distance from home (miles)	0	6	10	10	14	20

   (a) Draw a travel graph to show Tom's journey.

   (b) Estimate Tom's distance from home at **(i)** 8:05 **(ii)** 8:35.

3 Joseph cycles to his friend Beth's house. At the same time, Beth runs to Joseph's house. They do not see each other. Here is a travel graph of their journeys.

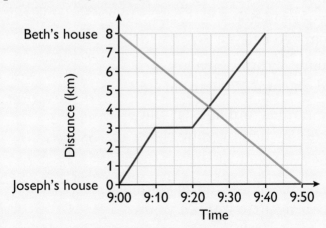

   (a) When do the two friends pass each other?

   (b) How far has Joseph travelled when he passes Beth?

   (c) Who travels faster? How can you tell?

Everyday graphs

Mercy's friend draws this graph.
It converts cats' ages to human ages.

Mercy's cat Tabby is 12 years old.

 How old is he in human years?

I cat year is
7 human years.

Mercy

 How steep is the slope?

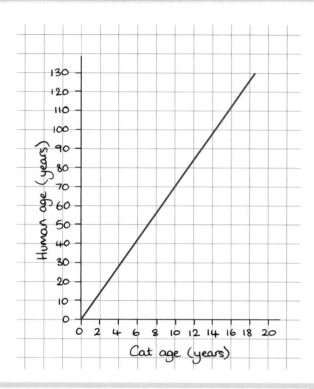

Task

Mercy gets a better graph from her vet.

The blue line converts dogs' ages to human ages.

The red line does the same for cats.

1 How old in human years is
  (a) an 8-year-old dog
  (b) a 2-year-old cat?

2 Which is older, in human years, a 10-year-old dog or a 17-year-old cat?

3 Collect the names and ages of the dogs and cats owned by your class.

4 Mark these on a copy of the graph.

5 List the pets, the oldest to the youngest, and add their ages, in human years.

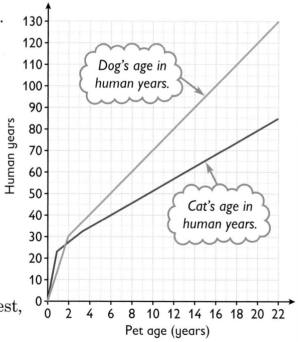

Dog's age in human years.

Cat's age in human years.

 Is it ever true that the human age of a dog is 7 times its real age?

 What about a cat?

Exercise

1 This graph shows the temperature
of water in a hot tub.
For each part of this story,
state the times.

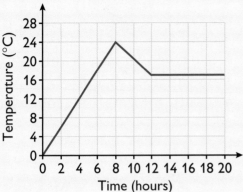

(a) The heater is turned on.

(b) The water reaches 24°C.
The heater is switched off.

(c) The water cools.

(d) Veronica puts the cover on.

(e) The water stays at a constant temperature.

2 This table shows the depth of water in a harbour one morning.

Time	04:00	05:00	06:00	07:00	08:00	09:00	10:00	11:00	12:00	13:00
Depth (m)	1.0	1.3	2.0	3.0	4.0	4.6	5.0	4.7	4.4	3.1

(a) Why does the depth change?

(b) Draw a graph of the depth against time. Join the points with
a smooth curve.

A ship needs 3.5 m of water to float.

(c) Use your graph to find out when the ship is afloat.

3 Land is measured in hectares or acres.
In this question, take 1 hectare to be 2.5 acres.

Copy and complete this table.

Hectares	0	5	10	15	20	25	30	35	40
Acres	0	12.5							

(a) Draw axes from 0 hectares to 40 hectares on the horizontal
axis and from 0 acres to 100 acres on the vertical axis.

(b) Draw a conversion graph.

(c) Use your graph to change
(i) 12 hectares into acres   (ii) 75 acres into hectares.

(d) Farmer Giles wants another field. Does he buy more land with
37 hectares or 80 acres?

Finishing off

Now that you have finished this chapter you should be able to:

- use a conversion graph
- use a travel graph
- obtain information from a graph of a real situation.

Review exercise

The Avonford Half-Marathon

1 This travel graph shows Thena's run when she took part in her local half-marathon.

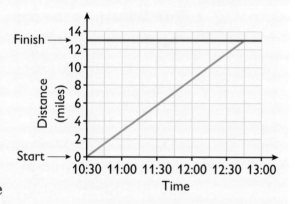

(a) Copy Thena's graph.

(b) When does the run start?

(c) When does Thena finish?

(d) How long does Thena take to finish?

(e) How far is the half-marathon?

2 Thena's friend Motol arrives late and starts at 10:45. After 30 minutes, he is 4 miles from the start. He meets a sick runner and stops to help him for 15 minutes. He finishes at 12:30.

(a) Add Motol's run to your graph.

(b) When does Motol overtake Thena?

(c) How far from the finish are they?

3 This table shows the conversion between miles and kilometres.

Miles	5	10	15	20	25	30
Kilometres	8	16	24	32	40	48

(a) Draw a conversion graph.

(b) How many kilometres is a half-marathon?

(c) How long is a full marathon in **(i)** miles **(ii)** kilometres?

4 This graph shows the number of spectators at the finishing point during the day.

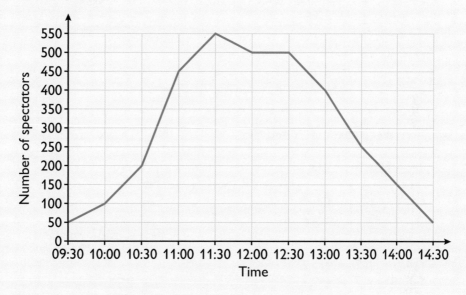

(a) What is the largest number of spectators?

(b) When is the crowd the largest?

(c) How many spectators are there at 2:00 pm?

(d) How big is the crowd when Thena finishes?

5 This table shows the temperature at Avonford on the day of the run.

Time	9:00	10:00	11:00	12:00	13:00	14:00	15:00
°C	16	17	19	22	26	30	29

(a) Draw a graph to shows this information.

(b) What is the temperature at the start of the run?

(c) What is the temperature when Thena finishes?

(d) When is the temperature 25 °C?

The four rules

Here is Ali's maths homework.

> **Q1** Find the sum of 486 and 137.
>
> $400 + 100 = 500$
> $80 + 30 = 110$
> $6 + 7 = 13$
>
> $500 + 110 + 13 = 623$
> So $486 + 137 = 623$ ✓
>
> **Q2** Find the difference between 354 and 168.
>
> $+200$　　-14
>
> 168　　368　　354
>
> $200 - 14 = 186$
> So $354 - 168 = 186$ ✓

? Explain Ali's working.

> **Q3** Find the product of 7 and 86.
>
> | | 80 | 6 |
> |---|----|---|
> | 7 | 7×80 = 560 | 7×6 = 42 |
>
> $560 + 42 = 602$
> So $86 \times 7 = 602$ ✓
>
> **Q4** Divide 276 by 6.
>
> I know　　$60 = 10 \times 6$
> So　　$120 = 20 \times 6$
> So　　$240 = 40 \times 6$
>
> 36 is still needed.
> I know　$36 = 6 \times 6$
>
> So $276 = 46 \times 6$
> So $276 \div 6 = 46$ ✓ Good work!

? Explain Ali's working.

Task

Work out these sums.
Match your answers to the letters to crack the code.

1 $356 + 248$　　**2** $487 - 259$　　**3** $392 \div 7$　　**4** $504 \div 9$
5 78×7　　**6** $357 - 269$　　**7** 182×3　　**8** $246 + 138$

A = 58	C = 384	E = 228	I = 546	F = 88
N = 572	P = 616	R = 56	S = 243	T = 604

? What other methods can you use to answer Ali's homework?

Exercise

1 Find the sum of these numbers.

(a) 746 and 219   (b) 429 and 96   (c) 386 and 413

2 Find the difference between these numbers.

(a) 516 and 419   (b) 731 and 419   (c) 825 and 543

3 Find the product of these numbers.

(a) 34 and 5   (b) 314 and 6   (c) 208 and 9

4 Work these out.

(a) $455 \div 7$ (b) $150 \div 6$ (c) $312 \div 8$

5 Jenny is working out how much money she spent last month.

(a) How much did Jenny spend?

(b) Jenny earns £1000 a month. How much does she have left?

Rent	£480
Food	£195
Clothes	£97
Travel	£64
Going Out	£82

6 Look how Lucy works out 19×24.

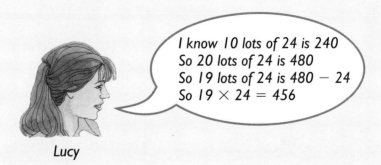

I know 10 lots of 24 is 240
So 20 lots of 24 is 480
So 19 lots of 24 is 480 − 24
So $19 \times 24 = 456$

Lucy

Work out the following using Lucy's method.

(a) 29×15 (b) 9×47 (c) 43×19

(d) 11×23 (e) 21×33 (f) 37×11

7 Humza and seven of his friends have gone out for a meal. The meal cost £184.

How much should each person pay?

Multiplication

Wayne and Michelle are working out how much Michelle earns a year from her Saturday job.

Look at their working.

Michelle's working

> This is **long multiplication**.

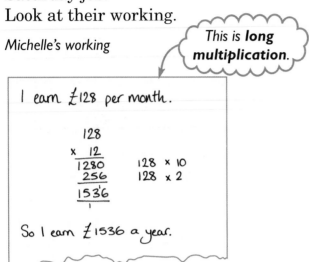

I earn £128 per month.

$$
\begin{array}{r}
128 \\
\times\ 12 \\
\hline
1280 \quad 128 \times 10\\
256 \quad 128 \times 2\\
\hline
1536 \\
\end{array}
$$

So I earn £1536 a year.

Wayne's working

> This is **partitioning**.

	100	20	8
10	100 × 10 = 1000	20 × 10 = 200	8 × 10 = 80
2	100 × 2 = 200	20 × 2 = 40	8 × 2 = 16

Michelle earns
£1000 + £200 + £80 + £200 + £40 + £16 = £1536

? **Explain both methods.**

? **Wayne earns £34 per week.**
How much does Wayne earn a year?

Task

1 Complete these multiplications.

(a)

$$
\begin{array}{r}
329 \\
\times\ 43 \\
\hline
13160 \quad 329 \times 40\\
{\scriptstyle 1\ 3}\\
+\ \underline{} \quad 329 \times 3\\
\hline
\\
\end{array}
$$

329 × 43 = ▢

(b)

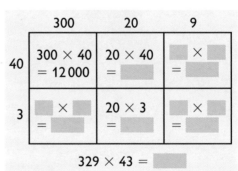

	300	20	9
40	300 × 40 = 12 000	20 × 40 = ▢	▢ × ▢ = ▢
3	▢ × ▢ = ▢	20 × 3 = ▢	▢ × ▢ = ▢

329 × 43 = ▢

2 Work out how much people receiving these amounts earn in a year.

(a) £45 per week   **(b)** £153 per month   **(c)** £53 per day

? **Which method do you like better? Why?**

Exercise

1 Work out the following.

(**a**) 24×27 (**b**) 52×16 (**c**) 73×12

(**d**) 64×17 (**e**) 126×13 (**f**) 13×139

2 Look at this advert.

(**a**) How much does it cost for one person to go to France?

(**b**) Calculate the cost for these groups of people.

(**i**) 12   (**ii**) 24   (**iii**) 45

> **SPEEDY TOURS**
> Day trip to France
> Coach £13
> Ferry £32
> Meal £18

3 A train has 16 coaches.
Each coach seats 64 people.
How many people can sit on the train?

4 A wood has 25 rows of trees.
Each row has 17 trees.
How many trees are there in the wood?

5 Look at this advert.

> **Avonford Ice Rink**
> £7 for one hour
> £5 skate hire

Calculate the cost for these groups of people.

(**a**) 15   (**b**) 25   (**c**) 35

6 A cinema has 37 rows of seats.
Each row seats 25 people.
How many people can watch a film at the same time?

7 A gardener plants   13 rows of 25 tulip bulbs
                       15 rows of 17 daffodil bulbs.

How many bulbs does he plant altogether?

Division

Jo and Andy are playing **Remainder bingo**.

They take a card from a pack and answer the question.
When the remainder is on their grid they can cross it off.
The winner is the first person to get a line of 3 crossed out.

Here are the first card and their grids.

427 ÷ 17

1	0	9
4	3	8
5	6	2

Jo's grid

7	0	10
6	1	4
3	2	8

Andy's grid

Look at Jo's working.

I know   17 × 10 = 170
So   17 × 20 = 340

I still need   427 − 340 = 87

I know   17 × 5 = 85   ← *Half of 170.*
So   17 × 25 = 340 + 85 = 425

So   425 ÷ 17 = 25
So   427 ÷ 17 = 25, remainder   ← **?**

? **What is the remainder? Who can cross off a number?**

? **25 × 13 = 325**
      What is the remainder when 325 is divided by (a) 13 (b) 25?

Task

1 Here are the next 4 cards.

260 ÷ 15		430 ÷ 13		172 ÷ 18		228 ÷ 12

Who wins?

2 Play your own game of **Remainder bingo** with a friend.

? **Check your answers on a calculator.**
      What do the answers on your calculator mean?

Exercise

1 Work these out.

    (a) $208 \div 13$

    (b) $260 \div 11$

    (c) $490 \div 15$

2 Millie is planning a trip for her
Youth Group.
She has £430 to spend.
How many people can go?

SPACE MUSEUM
Tickets £15 per person

3 326 students sign up for a school trip.
How many minibuses are needed?
Remember, **all** the students want to go!

Maximum
load
16 people

4 A group of friends go to Avonford Adventure Park.

Avonford Adventure Park
£24 per person

Total: £336

How many are in the group?

5 Mercy and Karl are working out $330 \div 12$.

    (a) What is $330 \div 12$?
        What is the remainder?

Mercy uses her calculator to check her answer.

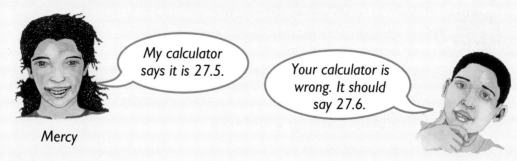

*My calculator
says it is 27.5.*

*Your calculator is
wrong. It should
say 27.6.*

Mercy

Karl

    (b) Who is right?
        Why?

Finishing off

Now that you have finished this chapter you should be able to:

- explain the meaning of the words **difference**, **product** and **sum**
- work out the difference, product and sum of two numbers
- divide a 3 digit number by a 2 digit number and find the remainder
- solve problems involving number calculations.

Review exercise

1　Find the sum of these numbers.

    (a) 321 and 123　　**(b)** 451 and 73　　**(c)** 285 and 472

2　Find the difference between these numbers.

    (a) 632 and 586　　**(b)** 327 and 115　　**(c)** 418 and 329

3　Find the product of these numbers.

    (a) 164 and 6　　**(b)** 21 and 18　　**(c)** 156 and 12

4　Work out these amounts.

    (a) $252 \div 7$　　**(b)** $247 \div 13$　　**(c)** $310 \div 14$

5　Avonford Town hire 9 coaches to take fans to an away match.
Each coach seats 56 people.
How many fans can go to the match?

6　In these number walls, each brick is found by adding together the
numbers in the two bricks underneath it.
Find the missing numbers.

(a)
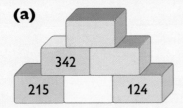

(b)
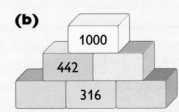

7 In these number pyramids, each brick is found by multiplying together the numbers in the two bricks underneath it.
Find the missing numbers.

(a)

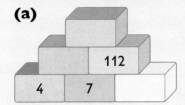

112

4 7

(b)

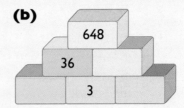

648

36

3

8 Avonford High School order new tables for the dining hall.
There is a choice of two designs.

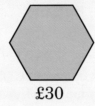 

£30   £32

The dining hall is to seat 336 students.

(a) How many **(i)** hexagonal **(ii)** octagonal tables does the school need?

(b) Which design of table is cheaper for the school to order? How much money does the school save?

Activity A Magic Product Square has the same product along each of its rows, column and diagonals.
This product is called the magic number.

I Look at this magic product square. Some of the numbers are missing.

12	9	2
		36

What is its magic number?

2 Find the missing numbers.

Symmetry review

The Hondo family are in France.

> Look at this house and garden. They are symmetrical.

? What symmetry can you see?

> Look at the paths. They are symmetrically placed. So are the benches.

? Name 2 other features that are symmetrical and 1 that is not.

Task

This garden has 2 lines of symmetry.

1 Complete the garden design.

2 Look at the middle part with the gravel and the flower-bed. How many lines of symmetry are there here?

	shrubs		seat		
		grass			
paving		bed			
		gravel			

? Describe the rotational symmetry of the windmill's sails.
Does the windmill have line symmetry?

Exercise

1 **(a)** Copy each of these shapes on to squared paper.
(b) Reflect it in the red line.

(i) **(ii)** 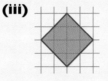 **(iii)**

2 **(a)** Copy these shapes.

(i) **(ii)** **(iii)** **(iv)** **(v)**

Draw in all their lines of symmetry.

(b) Write down the order of rotational symmetry for each shape.

3 Each of these diagrams shows
one quarter of a decorative brick.
Copy and complete the bricks by reflecting
first vertically and then horizontally.

(a) **(b)** **(c)**

4 **(a)** Copy this shape on to squared paper.
(b) On the same paper, draw if after
these rotations.

    (i) 90° anticlockwise about O
    (ii) 180° about O
    (iii) 90° clockwise about O.

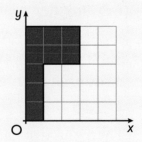

Activity Many is doing patchwork.
Here is her basic design.
Draw the basic design on squared paper.
On the same paper, draw it after these rotations.
(a) 90° about the corner C.
(b) Another 90°, still about C.
(c) Finally, another 90° about C.

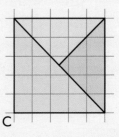

Translations review

Mandy is planning a
needlework design.
She begins like this.

Then she translates her design 6 squares to the right.

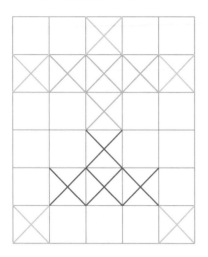
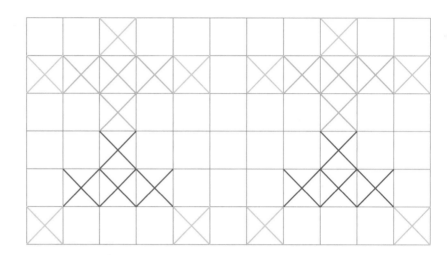

? **What does Mandy's design look like?**

Task

Another day, Mandy is
working on canvas using
long and short stitches.

1 Copy her design onto
   squared paper.

She translates this design
8 squares to the right.

2 Add this to your diagram.

Then she uses another colour
and translates the pattern
so far 4 squares to the
right and 2 squares up.

3 Draw this also.

4 How does she continue the pattern?

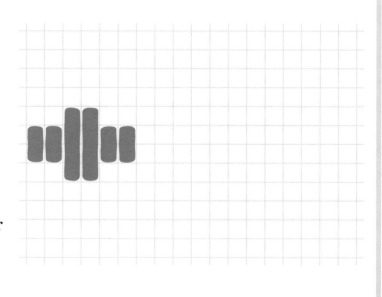

? **Where do you see translations in everyday life?**

Exercise

1 **(a)** Copy this shape on to squared paper.
Take x and y axes from -5 to 5.

(b) Draw the shape after:

(i) a translation of 4 to the right and 1 up

(ii) a translation of 2 to the left

(iii) a translation of 3 down

(iv) a translation of 6 down and 6 to the left.

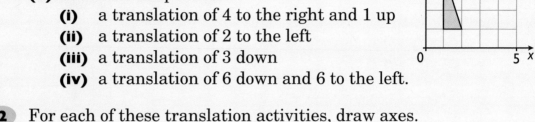

2 For each of these translation activities, draw axes.
Use 5 mm squared paper and take 1 cm to represent 2 units.
Number the x axis from -10 to $+10$.
Number the y axis from -4 to $+14$.

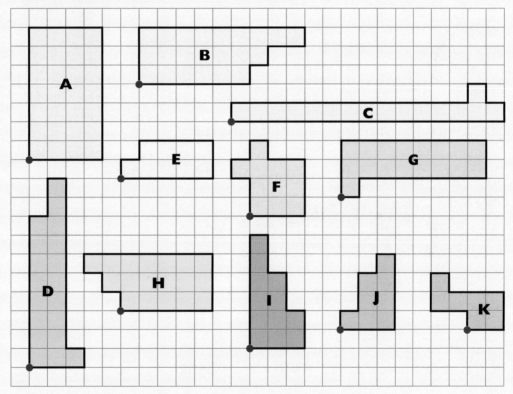

Trace each shape above and cut it out.

Place the corner marked with a dot on (0, 0).
Translate each shape as follows.

(i) A 0 across, 3 up

(ii) B 1 right, 4 down

(iii) C 5 left, 1 down

(iv) D 3 left, 2 up

(v) E 8 left, 2 up

(vi) F 0 across, 10 up

(vii) G 0 across, 0 up

(viii) H 4 left, 4 down

(ix) I 4 right, 3 up

(x) J 6 left, 4 up

(xi) K 8 left, 2 down

Enlargement

Look at this picture of a tunnel.

 How many rectangles are there?
How many points?

 A friend has not seen the picture.
Describe the picture to your friend.

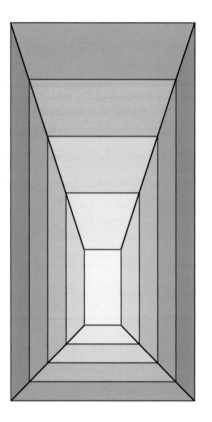

Measure the width and height of each rectangle in the tunnel picture.
Start with the smallest and end with the biggest.
Write your answers in a copy of this table.

Width	Height
1 cm	2 cm

 What can you say about the rectangles?

Now draw a copy of the tunnel for yourself.
Use squared paper.

Look at the smallest and largest rectangles in the picture.
The largest is an **enlargement** of the smallest.

 What is the scale factor of the enlargement?
Where is the centre of the enlargement?

Exercise

1 P is the centre of enlargement for each pair of shapes.
Find the scale factor of the enlargement in each case.

(a)

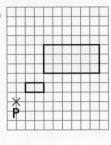

(b)

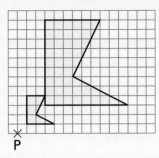

(c)

SU

2 **(a)** Copy these shapes onto squared paper.

(i)

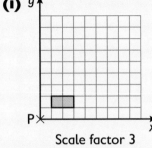

Scale factor 3

(ii)

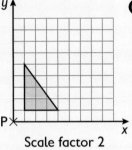

Scale factor 2

(iii)

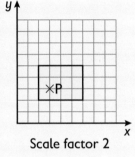

Scale factor 2

(b) Draw the image, using P as the centre of the enlargement.

Activity

Gary is a film star.
He chooses a photograph
to send to fans.

5 cm

4 cm

*This is too small.
Enlarge it.*

Gary

1 The photo is enlarged
by scale factor 2.
It is 8 cm high.
What is its length?

? cm

8 cm

2 The same picture can be printed in other sizes.
Copy and complete this table.

Photograph	Length	Height	Scale factor
Original	5 cm	4 cm	1
Fans		8 cm	2
Magazine	15 cm		
Poster	40 cm		

Finishing off

Now that you have finished this chapter you should be able to:

- understand symmetry of 2-dimensional shapes
- perform reflections, rotations, and translations
- enlarge shapes.

Review exercise

SU

1 On squared paper, reflect these in the axes shown in red.

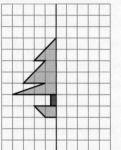 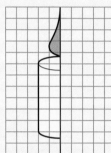 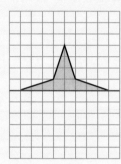 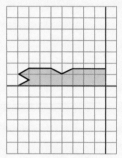

2 Decribe these translations.

    (a) A → C   **(b)** C → A

    (c) A → B   **(d)** B → A

    (e) A → D   **(f)** D → A

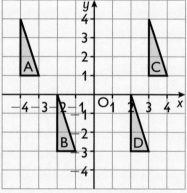

SU

3 **(a)** Copy these shapes on to squared paper.

    (b) Copy out these rotations on each shape. Draw the images.

      (i) 90° clockwise about O   **(ii)** 180° about O

      (iii) 90° anticlockwise about O

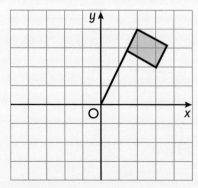 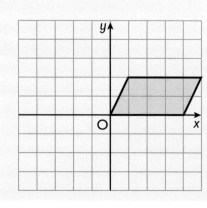

4 **(a)** Draw axes from −6 to +6.

(b) Plot the points (0, 0) (0, 4) (2, 6) and (2, 2).
Join them in order to form a parallelogram.

(c) Reflect this shape in the *y* axis.

(d) Reflect the whole design in the *x* axis.

(e) Rotate the whole design through 90° anticlockwise about (0, 0).

5 **(a)** On squared paper, copy these shapes.

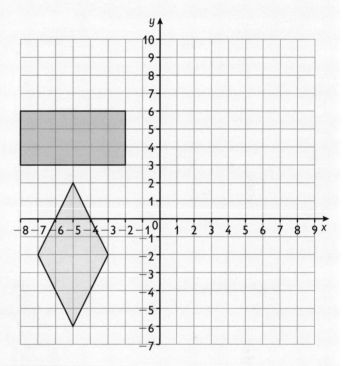

(b) Here are the co-ordinates of four more quadrilaterals.
Add them to your diagram.
(i) (7, 9) (9, 8) (7, 7) (0, 8)   **(ii)** (1, 5) (4, 3) (2, 0) (−1, 2)
(iii) (6, 4) (9, 2) (9, −3) (6, −1) **(iv)** (−2, −5) (6, −3) (4, −5) (6, −7)

(c) Name all the quadrilaterals you have drawn.

(d) Draw in the lines of symmetry.

(e) Inside each shape, write its order of rotational symmetry.

6 What is the order of rotational symmetry
of these windmills? (Ignore the mast.)
How many lines of symmetry does
each have?

Probability review

You have met these terms when studying probability.

Certain   **Probability scale**   **Likely**

Equally likely   **Evens**   **Estimate probability**

? Think of some more terms. Write a list of all the terms.
What do they all mean?

? The probability that a die will land on 3 is $\frac{1}{6}$.
How is this worked out?

? What is the probability that a die will land on an even number?

? Ginger has never tried Kitikins.
What is the probability
he will prefer it?

*7 out of
every 10 cats
prefer Kitikins
to other brands.*

Task

Make a biased coin.
Take a coin. Stick a small piece of plasticine on one side.
Toss the coin 100 times. Copy this table and add your results.

	Tally	Frequency
Heads		
Tails		

? Do you get the same number of heads and tails?

? Is your coin biased? Which way?

? Find an estimate for the probability that your coin lands heads.
Compare your results with the rest of the class.

Exercise

1 For each of these events, decide if the outcomes are equally likely. Answer 'equally likely' or 'not equally likely'.

Did you think of these terms when you made your list on page 176?

Event	Outcomes
(a) Throwing a fair die	1, 2, 3, 4, 5 or 6
(b) Firing an arrow	Scoring a bull's eye Hitting the target outside the bull Missing the target
(c) Waiting for a bus	The bus is early The bus is on time The bus is late

2 The table shows the coins in Kevin's pocket.

Coin	Frequency
10p	4
20p	3
50p	1
£1	2

(a) How many coins are in Kevin's pocket?

(b) Kevin pulls out a coin without looking.
Work out the probability that the coin is
  (i) a 10p
  (ii) a £1
  (iii) worth at least 50p
  (iv) worth more than 1p
  (v) worth more than £1

3 Copy these sentences about probability and fill in the blank spaces.

(a) Something that is ⬚ has a probability of 1.

(b) An impossible event has a probability of ⬚.

(c) A probability cannot be larger than ⬚.

(d) An event that is evens has a probability of ⬚.

(e) An event that is very likely has a ⬚ probability than an event that is likely.

Calculating probability

Harry and friends are playing Monopoly.
One of their dice is blue; the other is red.

I want to land on Bond Street. I need a total of 7.

You can get a 3 on the red die and a 4 on the blue die.

Harry

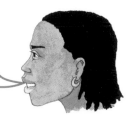

Christina

? **Is this the only way for Harry to throw 7?**

Task

Look at this table. It shows you the possible totals.

Red die

	1	2	3	4	5	6
1						
2						
3						
4			7			
5						
6						

Blue die (rows)

This 7 shows the total when the blue die lands on 4 and the red lands on 3.

1 Copy and complete the table.

2 There are 36 numbers in the table. How many of them are 7?

3 What is the probability that Jamie scores 7 on his turn?

? **Write a list of all the possible totals when you throw 2 dice.**

? **Are all the totals equally likely?**

? **What is the probability that the total is (a) 9   (b) 12   (c) 5?**

Exercise

1

Wheel of Fortune
Spin a star to win

(a) Make a list of the possible outcomes when you spin the wheel.

(b) Are the outcomes equally likely?

(c) How many stars are there?

(d) What is the probability that you spin a star?

(e) What is the probability that you spin a moon?

2 Ali plays monopoly.
She needs to throw a double to get out of jail.

> Both dice must have the same score.

Look at the table you prepared for the Task.

(a) Put a circle round the squares that show a double.

(b) Calculate the probability that Ali throws a double on her next turn.

3

Roll the die and toss the coin.
A head and an even number wins.

(a) Copy and complete this table to show the possible outcomes.

Die

		1	2	3	4	5	6
Coin	**Heads**	H1	H2				
	Tails	T1					

(b) How many outcomes are there?

(c) How many outcomes show a head and an even number?

(d) What is the probability that you win a prize?

(e) What is the probability that you do not win a prize?

Estimating probability

It always rains on my birthday, Mum.

Jack

It has rained on 8 of your last 10 birthdays.

 Use this information to estimate the probability that it will rain on Jack's next birthday.

Jack and his friends go to the fair.
They see this game.
They want to know the probability of winning.

Throw 2 coins 2 heads or 2 tails win.
YOU CAN'T LOSE.

 Task

The tally chart records the outcomes when you toss 2 coins.

Outcome	Tally	Frequency
2 tails		
A head and a tail		
2 heads		

Toss 2 coins 20 times.
Record the outcomes on a copy of this tally chart.
Complete the frequency column.

1 Are the outcomes equally likely?

2 Which outcome happens most?

3 Use your results to estimate the probability of each outcome.

4 What is the probability of winning the game?

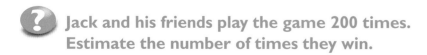 Jack and his friends play the game 200 times.
Estimate the number of times they win.

Exercise

1

Kim's Dad

Why does toast always land butter side down?

I've dropped this piece 10 times. It has landed butter side down 7 times.

Kim

(a) Estimate the probability that the next piece of toast that Kim drops lands butter side down.

(b) Kim drops the toast 100 times. It lands butter side down 65 times.
Make a new estimate for the probability that the next piece lands butter side down.

(c) Which estimate is better?

2 Mark fires an arrow 50 times.
Here are the results.

Outcome	Frequency
Bull's eye	10
Hit target outside the bull	25
Miss the target	15

(a) Estimate the probability that Mark scores a bull's eye with his next shot.

(b) Estimate the probability that Mark's next arrow misses the target.

(c) Mark fires an arrow 100 times. Estimate the number of bull's eyes he gets.

Activity

Not a complete pack.

Work with a friend. You need some playing cards.
Ask your friend to choose one of the cards.
Is the card red?
Put the card back and ask your friend to choose again.
Repeat this 10 times. How many times does your friend choose a red card?
Estimate the probability that the next card chosen is red.
Do you have more red cards or more black cards?

Swap with your friend and repeat the experiment.
Do you get the same results?

Finishing off

Now that you have finished this chapter you should be able to:
● use the language of probability
● calculate simple probabilities
● use the results of an experiment to estimate probabilities.

Review exercise

1 Samir has 10 socks in his drawer. 4 are red, 2 blue and 4 black. He takes a red sock out.

(a) How many socks are left in the drawer?

(b) How many red socks are left in the drawer?

(c) What is the probability that the next sock Samir takes out is red?

2 Sophie comes to school on the bus.
She records the number of times she is late, on time or early for 20 days.

Late   4
On time   11
Early   5

Estimate the probability that on the next day Sophie is

(a) late

(b) on time

(c) not late.

3 Lee is a goalkeeper. He saves 11 out of 20 penalties.

(a) Estimate the probability that Lee saves the next penalty.

(b) Estimate the probability that the next penalty scores a goal.

(c) Estimate how many of the next 40 penalties Lee saves.

4 The table shows the outcomes when both spinners are spun.

Blue spinner

	1	2	3	4	5
1					
2					
3					
4					

Red spinner

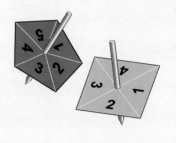

(a) Copy and complete the table to show the total of the two spinners.

(b) How many outcomes are there?

(c) How many outcomes give a score of 6?

(d) What is the probability of scoring 6?

(e) What is the probability of scoring 9?

(f) Which score has the highest probability?

Activity Work with a friend.
Throw 2 dice 120 times.

Record your results on a bar chart like this.

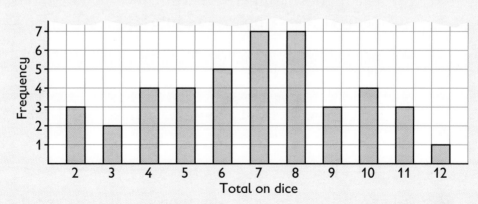

Colour in a square each time you score that number.

(a) Which score has the highest frequency?

(b) Estimate the probability of this score.

(c) Compare your results with the rest of the class.

(d) Make a class poster to show your results.

The four rules

1. (a) What number do you add to 28 to make 132?

   (b) What number do you subtract from 132 to make 85?

   (c) What number do you multiply by 15 to make 105?

   (d) What number do you divide by 6 to make 12?

2. (a) Sarah pays £16.20 to travel to work each week. She works 45 weeks each year.
      How much does it cost her to travel to work each year?
      Show your working.

   (b) She can buy a season ticket for the whole year. It costs £630.
      How much is that per week? Show your working.

3. The diagram shows how to change temperatures in °F into °C.

   | °F | → | Subtract 32 | → | Multiply by 5 | → | Divide by 9 | → | °C |

   (a) The highest temperature ever recorded in a human is 115.7 °F.
      Convert this temperature into °C.

   (b) Copy the following and fill in the boxes to show how to change from °C into °F.

   | °C | → | ☐ | → | ☐ | → | ☐ | → | °F |

4. Edwards wants to work out approximate answers for these sums.
   Copy the sums and fill in the gaps.

   (a) $679 + 645 \approx 700 + \boxed{} = \boxed{}$

   (b) $47 \times 62 \approx 50 \times \boxed{} = \boxed{}$

   (c) $311 \div 29 \approx 300 \div \boxed{} = \boxed{}$

Fractions and percentages

1

Look at the 10 animals.

(a) What fraction of the animals are cats?

(b) Write this as a decimal.

(c) What fraction are dogs? Write this in the simplest form.

(d) What percentage are rabbits?

2 Fill in the boxes.

(a) $\frac{1}{2} \times 58 =$ ☐

(b) $\frac{1}{4} \times$ ☐ $= 10$

(c) ☐ $\times 12 = 4$

3 What percentage of each diagram is shaded?

(a)

(b)

(c)

4 An adult weighs 80 kg. 60% of his total mass is water.
What is the mass of this water?

5

The new bar is 20% bigger than the old bar.
How much does the new bar weigh?

Decimals

1 Copy the numbers.
Match the decimal with an equivalent number.
The first one has been done.

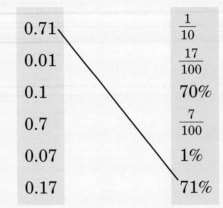

$$0.71 \qquad \frac{1}{10}$$
$$0.01 \qquad \frac{17}{100}$$
$$0.1 \qquad 70\%$$
$$0.7 \qquad \frac{7}{100}$$
$$0.07 \qquad 1\%$$
$$0.17 \qquad 71\%$$

2 Copy and complete the following calculations.

(a) $0.4 + 0.05 = \boxed{}$

(b) $\boxed{} \times 2 = 0.14$

(c) $4.5 - \boxed{} = 1.3$

(d) $2.4 \div 3 = \boxed{}$

3 The 2 small tins weigh the same.
The weight of the big tin is 2.6 kg.
What is the weight of one small tin?
Show your working.

4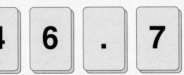

Rearrange the cards to make this number
(a) ten times bigger
(b) ten times smaller.

5 Harry puts decimals in ascending order. Which of these are correct?

(a)	0.2	0.12	0.21	0.22
(b)	3.7	3.73	3.3	7.3
(c)	1.06	1.6	1.66	6.1

Ratio and proportion

1 Jo makes a chocolate cake.
She wants to make it for 12 people.
Work out how much of each ingredient she needs
using the information below.

   (a) 1 egg for every 3 people

   (b) 100 g of flour for every egg

   (c) Half as much sugar as flour

   (d) 10 g of margarine for every person

   (e) Half as much again chocolate as margarine.

2 Copy and complete the following.

   (a) $3 : 6 = \boxed{} : 2$

   (b) $6 : 21 = 2 : \boxed{}$

   (c) $\boxed{} : 15 = 1 : 3$

3

50 sweets are shared out equally between these children.

   (a) How many sweets do the girls get?

   (b) In what ratio are the sweets shared between the boys and the girls?

4 The diagrams are **similar**. Work out the missing lengths.

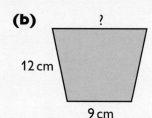

(a) 5 cm   ?   3 cm

(b) ?   12 cm   9 cm

Special numbers

1 Copy the table and fill in each box.
The first row is done for you.

	Is it a square number?	Is it a multiple of 3?	Is it a prime number?	Is it a factor of 100
64	Yes	No	No	No
9				
25				
27				
17				

2 Copy and complete these.

(a) $4^2 =$ ▢

(b) ▢$^3 = 125$

(c) $2^▢ = 16$

3 When the wind blows it feels colder. Fill in the gaps in a copy of the table. The first row is done for you.

	Temperature out of the wind	How much colder it feels in the wind	Temperature it feels in the wind
Moderate breeze	5	7 degrees colder	-2
Fresh breeze	-8	11 degrees colder	▢
Strong breeze	-4	▢ degrees colder	-20
Gale	▢	23 degrees colder	-45

4 Copy and fill in the boxes.

(a) $(-4) + (-4) =$ ▢

(b) $8 -$ ▢ $= -2$

(c) ▢ $+ (-5) = 3$

Algebra

1   When $x = 4$, work out the values of these expressions.

(a) $x + 7$ (b) $x - 3$

(c) $2x$ (d) $2x + 4$

(e) $10 - 2x$ (f) $4 + 3x$

2   Karl has m marbles.
Michelle has 5 more marbles than Karl.

(a) Write down an expression for the number
of marbles Michelle has.

Lucy has twice as many marbles as Michelle.

(b) Which of these expressions give the number of marbles that
Lucy has?

$2m + 5$	$2(m + 5)$	$10 + m$	$2m + 10$

Lucy has 30 marbles.

(c) How many marbles does Karl have?

3   (a) Solve these equations to find the values of a, b and c.

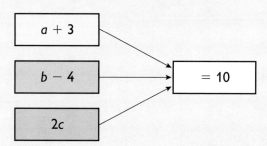

(b) Solve these equations to find the values of a, b and c.

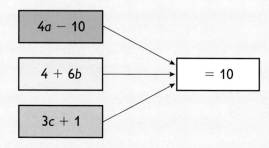

4 A boat hire company uses these formulae to work out costs.

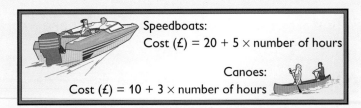

Speedboats:
Cost (£) = 20 + 5 × number of hours

Canoes:
Cost (£) = 10 + 3 × number of hours

(a) How much does it cost to hire a speedboat for 4 hours?

(b) How much does it cost to hire a canoe for 3 hours?

(c) How much more does it cost to hire a speedboat for 5 hours than a canoe?

5 This is a sequence of patterns with red and blue tiles.

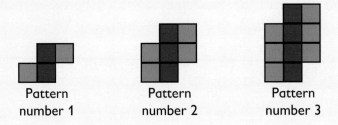

Pattern number 1   Pattern number 2   Pattern number 3

(a) Draw pattern number 4.

(b) Copy and complete this table.

Pattern number	Number of red tiles	Number of blue tiles
1	2	2
2	3	4
3		
4		
10		
20		

(c) Think about pattern n.
Write down expressions for the number of

(i) red tiles

(ii) blue tiles

(iii) tiles in total.

Give your answers as simply as possible.

Graphs

1 Jan runs The Pink Parsnip café.
She keeps a record of sales of coffee for 10 weeks.

Week	1	2	3	4	5	6	7	8	9	10
Sales	200	150	100	150	250	350	200	250	200	150

(a) Copy the axes and draw a graph to show Jan's sales data.

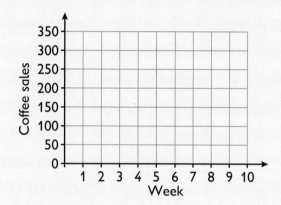

(b) Jan's best week for coffee sales was when the Fair was in town.
Which week was that?

2 Look at this diagram.

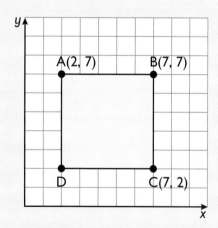

(a) Shape ABCD is a square.
What are the co-ordinates of point D?

(b) Which of the points A, B, C and D are on these lines?

    (i) $x = 2$ **(ii)** $x = 7$ **(iii)** $y = 7$

    (iv) $y = 2$ **(v)** $y = x$ **(vi)** $x + y = 9$

3 **(a)** Copy and complete this table of values for $y = x + 3$.

x	0	1	2	3	4	5
+3	+3	+3				
$y = x + 3$	+3	+4				

(b) Draw x and y axes, each from 0 to 10.
Use your table of values to draw the graph of $y = x + 3$.

(c) Copy and complete this table of values for $y = 2x$.

x	0	1	2	3	4	5
$y = 2x$						

(d) Draw the graph of $y = 2x$ on the same axes as **(b)**.

(e) What are the co-ordinates of the point where $y = 2x$ and $y = x + 3$ cross?

4

Avonford Leisure Centre
Non-members: Use of pool **£2.00**

(a) Copy and complete this table of values for customers using the swimming pool.

Number of visits	0	5	10	15	20	25	30
Total cost (£)	0	10					

(b) Show the information in the table as a graph.

(c)

Avonford Leisure Centre
Fitness Club
Membership £20 per year
Use of pool £1 per visit

Copy and complete this table of costs for members of the Fitness Club.

Number of visits	0	5	10	15	20	25	30
Total cost (£)	20	25					

(d) Show the Fitness Club information on the same graph as in **(b)**.

(e) Humza joins the Fitness Club. He uses the pool twice a week.
After how many weeks does he save money?

Geometry

1 On centimetre squared paper

(a) draw a **rectangle** that has an area of $12\,\text{cm}^2$

(b) draw a **different** rectangle that has an area of $12\,\text{cm}^2$.

(c) What is the perimeter of each rectangle in (a) and (b)?

(d) Draw a **triangle** that has an area of $6\,\text{cm}^2$.

2 This diagram shows a box.

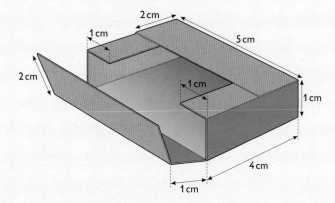

On centimetre squared paper, draw the net for the box.

3 Look at this diagram.

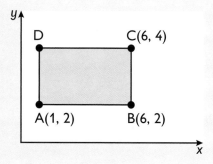

(a) A point K is half way between points B and C.
What are the co-ordinates of point K?

(b) Shape ABCD is a **rectangle**.
What are the co-ordinates of point D?

4 Look at these shapes.

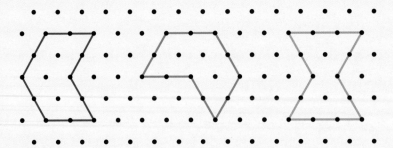

(a) Explain why all the shapes are **hexagons**.

(b) On an isometric grid, draw a **regular hexagon**.

5 Use a ruler and compasses to construct a triangle that has sides 10 cm, 8 cm and 7 cm.

6 Look at the hexagon and the triangle.

(a) Do the hexagon and the triangle have the same area? How do you know?

(b) Do the hexagon and the triangle have the same perimeter? How do you know?

7 This is a sketch plan of a ferry crossing. It is not drawn accurately.

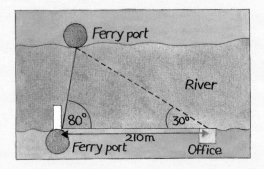

(a) Using a scale of 1 cm to 20 m, construct an accurate scale drawing of the ferry crossing.

(b) What is the length of the ferry crossing on your diagram?

(c) Work out the length of the real ferry crossing.

8 **(a)** A shape has 4 straight sides.
All 4 sides are the same length.
It has 4 right angles.
Draw the shape. What is it?

(b) A different shape has 4 straight sides.
It has 2 pairs of parallel sides.
It has 4 right angles.
Draw this shape. What is it?

(c) A shape has 4 straight sides.
It has 2 pairs of parallel sides.
It has no right angles.
Draw this shape. What is it?

9 Look at this diagram, which is not drawn accurately.
Triangle ABD is the reflection of triangle ABC in the line AB.

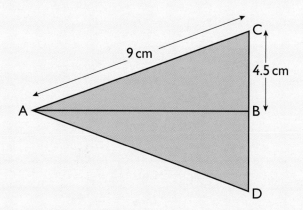

(a) Fill in the gaps. The first one has been done for you.

(i) The length of AC is 9 cm.

(ii) The length of AD is ____ cm.

(iii) The length of CD is ____ cm.

(b) What is the special name for triangle ACD?

Displaying data

1 These are the sandwiches David sells one lunch time.

> Cheese, ham, salad, cheese, ham, ham, chicken, salad, chicken, salad, cheese, ham, ham, chicken, salad, prawn, cheese, prawn, salad, ham

(a) Copy and complete this tally chart to show David's sandwich sales.

Sandwich type	Tally	Frequency
Cheese		
Ham		
Salad		
Chicken		
Prawn		

(b) Draw a bar chart to show David's sales.

(c) Which type is most popular?

2 This pictogram shows the colours of cars in a car park.

Colour of car	Frequency
red	
blue	
white	
silver	
green	

= 2 cars

(a) How many white cars are there?

(b) What does this symbol mean?

(c) How many red cars are there?

(d) How many cars are in the car park?

3 This 2-way table shows the languages studied by Year 9 students.

	Language		
	French	German	Spanish
Boys	10	14	6
Girls	21	7	14

(a) How many girls study Spanish?

(b) How many boys study a language?

(c) How many students study German?

4 Mary has drawn a stem and leaf diagram to show the length of the phone calls she makes one week.

Stem	Leaf
0	2 4 4 5
1	0 2 5 5 6 7 8
2	1 3 4
3	1 2 5 9
4	7

Key: 1 | 2 means 12 minutes

(a) How long is the shortest call?

(b) How long is the longest call?

(c) How many calls does Mary make?

(d) What is the median length?

Averages

1   Find the mode and median of these sets of data.

　　(a) 1, 2, 4, 4, 5, 7, 9, 10, 12

　　(b) 9, 9, 5, 12, 17, 10, 9, 12, 10

2   Calculate the mean of these sets of data.

　　(a) 10, 9, 5, 12, 7

　　(b) 21, 12, 14, 6, 20, 9, 5, 10

3

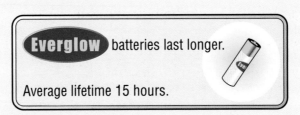

Everglow batteries last longer.

Average lifetime 15 hours.

Here are the lifetimes of 10 batteries.

> 15 hours, 19 hours, 12 hours, 15 hours, 10 hours,
> 17 hours, 6 hours, 16 hours, 9 hours, 8 hours

　　(a) Find the mean lifetime for the batteries.

　　(b) Find the median lifetime for the batteries.

　　(c) Is the claim correct?

　　(d) Which average have you used?

4   Here are the points scored by two rugby teams in 10 matches.

Team	Scores
Avonford Wanderers	11, 6, 9, 21, 15, 21, 16, 12, 3, 12
Bexley Lions	0, 24, 7, 18, 5, 8, 9, 12, 9, 22

　　(a) Calculate the mean score for each team.

　　(b) Find the range for each team.

　　(c) Which team has the better scores?

Probability

1 The sentences below have words missing.
Find the missing word for each sentence.

   (a) It is ____ that the sun will rise tomorrow.

   (b) The probability that a lost glove is for the right hand is ____ .

   (c) A fair coin is ____ ____ to land heads or tails.

   (d) It is ____ that you will learn to drive a car.

   (e) It is ____ that you will win a lottery prize this weekend.

   (f) The ____ of throwing a 3 is $\frac{1}{6}$.

   (g) I must use an ____ to estimate the probability that this drawing pin will land point up.

   (h) It is ____ that an athlete will run a mile in less than 1 minute.

2 Sam plants 10 tomato seeds.
8 grow into tomato plants.

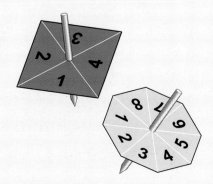

   (a) Estimate the probability that the next seed Sam plants will grow into a plant.

   (b) Sam plants 35 more seeds.
   Estimate the number that will grow.

3

Blue

	1	2	3	4	5	6	7	8
1	2	3						
2								
3								
4								

Red

The table shows the totals when the spinners are spun.

   (a) Fill in the totals on a copy of the table. The first 2 have been done for you.

   (b) There are 32 numbers in the table. How many of them are 12?

   (c) What is the probability that the total is 12?

   (d) Write a list of all the possible totals.

   (e) Find the probability of all the totals in your list for part **(d)**.

Having a job

There's some overtime on Saturday and Sunday if you want it.

Rob's boss

I could do with the extra money. Overtime pays time-and-a-half doesn't it?

Rob

Rob is 17. His basic rate of pay is the minimum wage for 16- and 17-year-old workers.

 What is the minimum wage?

 What does 'time-and-a-half' mean?

 Task

This is Rob's time sheet for a week at work.

Castlegate Construction Company							
Name R. Floyd		*Clock No.* 32			*Dept.* Electrical		
Work site	**Mon**	**Tues**	**Wed**	**Thur**	**Fri**	**Sat**	**Sun**
Smith's Outfitters Ltd	5		2				
Jubilee Walk site	2	7	3				
33 Arnside Grove			2	3			
Highland Food Company				4		3	2
Supersave Offices					7		

1 How many hours does Rob work in his basic week, Monday to Friday?
2 What is Rob's basic wage per hour?
3 What is Rob's basic wage for a 35-hour week?
4 How much does Rob earn for 1 hour's overtime?
5 How much overtime does he work this week?
6 How much overtime pay does he earn this week?

Rob gets the single person's tax allowance.

 What does this mean? Does he have to pay tax?

Exercise

This is part of an old pay slip.
At the time, Rob's tax code is 461. This means that the first £4610 he earns is tax free.

Castlegate Construction Company					
Robert Floyd 12 Audrey Close Middlesbrough	EMPLOYEE REF 021		N.I. NUMBER AB123456C	N.I. CAT	DATE 31/06/04
	TAX CODE 461		TAX PERIOD 30	TAX REF	TAX YEAR 2003/04
PAYMENTS	UNIT	RATE	TOTAL	N.I.	P.A.Y.E.
BASIC HOURS	35	3.00	105.00		
OVERTIME	5	4.50	22.50		
HOLIDAYS	0		00.00		

1 **(a)** What is Rob's basic wage for a week?

(b) How much overtime does he earn?

(c) What is his total pay for the week?

2 Rob is paid the minimum wage during his 4-week holiday.

(a) How much is his basic pay for one year?

(b) He averages 5 hours' overtime every working week. How much overtime pay does he get in one year?

(c) What is his total pay for the year?

Activity Now Rob is 18 years old, his pay has increased to the minimum wage for workers aged 18 to 21. Complete a copy of this pay slip for Rob's 35-hour week with overtime.

Castlegate Construction Company					
Robert Floyd 12 Audrey Close Middlesbrough	EMPLOYEE REF 021		N.I. NUMBER AB123456C	N.I. CAT	DATE
	TAX CODE 464		TAX PERIOD 30	TAX REF	TAX YEAR 2004/05
PAYMENTS	UNIT	RATE	TOTAL	N.I.	P.A.Y.E.
BASIC HOURS	35				
OVERTIME	5				
HOLIDAYS	0				

Having a bank account

Rob's company pays his wages straight into his bank account.
He uses the ATM to withdraw money from his account each week.

*ATM stands for
Automatic Tell Machine –
a cash machine*

 What is to stop someone else taking Rob's money out of the machine?

Task

This is part of Rob's bank book. It shows his Current Account details.

Date	Cheque	Description	Money out	Money in	Balance Brought Forward £13 50
					Balance
7 Mar		Castlegate Construction		£128 00	£141 50
8 Mar		ATM	£50 00		£91 50
8 Mar	1232	N.U.F.C.	£30 00		
13 Mar	1233	Football club	£7 50		
14 Mar		Castlegate Construction		£147 20	
15 Mar	1234	Complete Clothing Co.			

1 Complete the Balance column on a copy of his record.

2 Enter the following details to bring his record up to date.
   On 15 March Rob used cheques to buy
   (a) a pair of jeans from Complete Clothing Company for £44.99
   (b) two DVDs from Super CDs Record Shop for £29.98
   (c) a pair of trainers from Multi-Sport at £79.99.
   On 22 March he used the ATM to withdraw £50.

 What is the difference between a Credit Card and a Debit Card?

 What is the difference between a Current Account and a Savings Account?

Exercise

Rob's bank sends him a statement each month.
It shows what has happened to his account.

This is part of Rob's statement.

Account No 1234567	Current Limit 1000		Telephone 01234-567890 Date 6 April	
Date	**Details**	**Debits**	**Credits**	**Balance**
8 MAR	ATM	50 00		91 50
8 MAR	TRANSFER	30 00		61 50
10 MAR	DD ELECTRICIANS UNION	5 00		56 50
14 MAR	CASTLEGATE		147 20	203 70
21 MAR	CASTLEGATE		147 20	350 90
24 MAR	1235	29 98		323 92
26 MAR	1233	7 50		316 42

1 **(a)** Why does Rob need to check his statement when he gets it?

(b) What does DD ELECTRICIANS UNION mean?

(c) What does TRANSFER mean?

(d) List some of the differences between Rob's bank statement and the bank book details from the Task.

Activity Complete a copy of the cheque Rob wrote when he bought a pair of jeans, costing £44.99 from The Complete Clothing Company.

1 What does A/C PAYEE mean?

2 What do these three numbers mean?

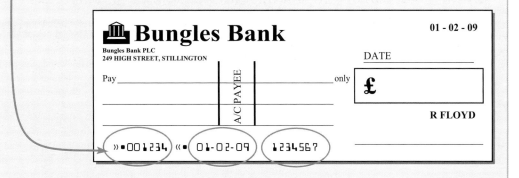

Going on holiday

Rob and Pete are planning a holiday in Belfast.

Lagan Hotel

Number of nights	2	3	4	5
1 Oct–31 Oct	199	234		
1 Nov–31 Dec	193	226		
1 Jan–29 Feb	204	239		
1 Mar–25 May	212	247		
26 May–30 Jun	222	262		

B&B prices based on two people sharing and including return flights and transfers.

Additional nights £35 pppn

pppn means per person per night.

1 (a) What does B&B mean?

(b) What does 'return flights' mean?

(c) What does 'including transfers' mean?

2 Between which dates is the most expensive holiday?

3 On a copy of the brochure table, fill in the prices for 4-night and 5-night holidays.

A 2-night holiday costs £199.

 Why does a 4-night holiday not cost double this price?

 Why is a holiday cheaper during December than October?

Exercise

Pete looks up holidays on the Internet. He finds hotel and flight prices in £.

HOTEL PRICES

DUBLIN BAY HOTEL	£
1 Oct – 31 Oct	60
1 Nov – 31 Dec	55
1 Jan – 29 Feb	60
1 Mar – 25 May	65
26 May – 30 Jun	70
1 July – 31 Aug	75

Prices per twin room per night GB£.

SUN AIR   **DUBLIN FLIGHTS**

DATE	Return flight £
1 Oct – 31 Oct	55
1 Nov – 31 Dec	80
1 Jan – 29 Feb	60
1 Mar – 25 May	65
26 May – 30 Jun	45
1 July – 31 Aug	60

Prices include all taxes but **not** transfers.

SUN AIR coach transfer £10 return.

1 How much does a room cost for 3 nights from 14 April?

2 How much does a flight cost for each person from 14 April?

3 What is the total cost for each person of a 3 night holiday from 14 April?

Don't forget transfers!

4 Rob and Pete each have £180 to pay for their flights, transfer and room. Have they enough money for a 4-night holiday in December?

5 Why are hotel prices more expensive in July and August?

Activity   Work out the total cost of a 4-night stay for 2 people in Dublin during August.

1 Goal chains

Avonford Star

2-1 winners. Avonford heroes lift the cup.

The final score is Avonford 2 Barford 1, but look how it changed through the match.

Time (minutes)	Event	Score
0	Kick-off	0–0
1	Barford score a penalty after trip on striker Lee Jones	0–1
72	Avonford score through long distance shot by Dave Carter	1–1
90	Last-minute header from Steve Rew puts Avonford ahead	2–1

Look at the way the score changes.

0–0   0–1   1–1   2–1

This is a goal chain.
You can draw a goal chain
on a graph.

Here is another possible goal chain
for this match.

0–0   1–0   2–0   2–1

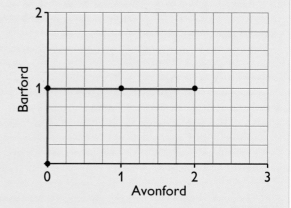

1 Draw a graph of this goal chain.

There is another possible goal chain
for the score 2–1.

2 Find this goal chain and draw it on your graph. Use a different colour.

You are going to investigate goal chains.

3 Look at these scores.

| 1–0 | 2–0 | 3–0 | 1–1 | 2–1 | 3–1 | 2–2 | 3–2 |

(a) Count the number of chains for each score.

(b) Draw graphs of the chains.

(c) Make up a table of your results like this.

Score	Number of chains
1–0	
2–0	
3–0	
1–1	
2–1	
3–1	
2–2	
3–2	

4 Look for patterns in the table.
Write them down.

5 Use the patterns in your table to predict the number of goal chains for these scores.

(a) 4–0

(b) 4–1

(c) 4–2

6 Find all the chains for question **5**, and so check your answers.

7 The first team scores g goals.
Use algebra to write your rules for the number of goal chains when the score is

(a) g–0

(b) g–1

(c) g–2

② **Doing a survey**

The government is worried that today's children are unhealthy. This is because of poor diet and not enough exercise.

You are going to carry out a survey.
Write a questionnaire to find out if the pupils in your school
• eat a healthy diet
• take enough exercise.

1 Decide who to give your questionnaire to.

We should ask the whole school.

That will take too long.

Just Year 9 then.

We must ask different age groups.

Alan

Sophie

2 You need some questions about what pupils eat.

Tim

Everybody should eat at least 5 portions of fruit and vegetables a day.

(a) Write a question to find out how many portions of fruit and vegetables are eaten.

We eat too many chips.

(b) Write a question to find out how many times pupils eat chips or fried food.

Lucy

3 You need to find out about what pupils drink.

Too many fizzy drinks are causing tooth decay.

It is healthy to drink 2 litres of water each day.

Write 2 questions to find out this information.

4 You need to find out about exercise.

Mercy

You should exercise for $\frac{1}{2}$ hour 5 times a week.

I walk to school everyday.

Tim

(a) Write a question to find out how often pupils exercise.

(b) Write a question to find out the type of exercise they take.

I cycle. Cycling is best for keeping you fit.

Wayne

5 Try your questionnaire on a small group first.

Sophie

I don't understand this question.

There isn't a space for my answer.

Alan

6 Change any questions that are hard to answer.

7 Carry out your survey.

8 Draw graphs to show the results of your survey.

Lucy

Should I use a bar chart or a pie chart?

A pictogram can show the different types of exercise.

Mercy

9 Find averages for some of your results.

Tim

Find the mean number of portions of fruit and vegetables that are eaten.

What is the most popular type of exercise?

Sophie

10 Do your results show that medical workers are right to be worried?

11 Design a poster to persuade pupils in your school to be more healthy. Use your results in your poster.

Pupils spend an average of 5 hours a day watching television.

More than 60% of pupils eat chips every day.

3 Circles

Raj has a new bicycle.

I wonder how many times the wheels will go round if I cycle for 1 km?

If you know the diameter of the wheel, then you can find the circumference.

Raj

Kate

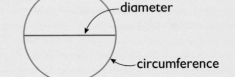

diameter

circumference

1 What is the diameter of a circle?

2 What is the circumference?

3 How could you measure the circumference of a circle?

Try these two methods.

Method A

1 Wind a piece of string or wool round a circular object.

2 Unwind the string and measure the length.

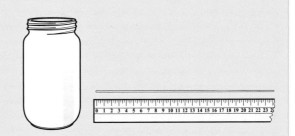

Method A

1 Make a mark on the circumference of the circular object.

2 Lay a tape measure along the table.

3 Start with the mark at 0 on the tape, then roll the object along the tape until you reach the mark again.

4 Read the measurement off the tape.

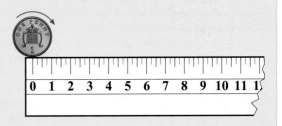

Collect some circular objects, for example coins, jars, tins, cardboard tubes, mugs.

For each object, make two measurements.
First use a ruler to measure the diameter.

Remember, the diameter is the distance across the circle through its centre.

Now use one of the methods to measure the circumference of each object.

Put the measurements all together in a table like this.

Object	Diameter	Circumference	$C \div D$
2p coin			
jam jar lid			

Circumference divided by Diameter.

1 What do you find?
Copy and complete this rule.

Now I can answer my question.

Raj

The circumference of a circle is
always approximately   × diameter.

Raj measures the diameter of his bicycle wheel.
It is 50 cm.

2 Approximately what is the circumference of the wheel?

3 How far does the bicycle travel when the wheel turns 10 times?
100 times?

4 How many times does it turn to travel 1 km?

Remember: 100 cm = 1 m and 1000 m = 1 km

5 Work out the answer to Raj's question.

6 Write a **report** on your work. Say what you did and what you found.

Include all your measurements, diagrams and ideas, and the answer to Raj's question.

Write a sentence to **summarise** what you found out about circles.

Answers

Here are the answers to the 'Finishing off' review exercises to help you check your progress. All other answers are in the Teacher's Resource that goes with this book.

1   Units (pages 10–11)
1 **(a)** 10 m
   (b) Yes (200 mm spare)
   (c) 250 mm on both sides
2 **(a)** 35 g, 45 g, 150 g, 750 g, 1.4 kg, 2.3 kg
   (b) 935 g
   (c) No (the rest of the fish total 2.38 kg)
3

A

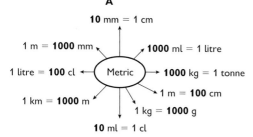

10 mm = **1** cm

1 m = **1000** mm   **1000** ml = 1 litre

1 litre = **100** cl ←   Metric   → **1000** kg = 1 tonne

1 km = **1000** m   1 m = **100** cm

                          1 kg = **1000** g

10 ml = **1** cl

B

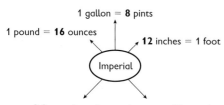

1 gallon = **8** pints

1 pound = **16** ounces

                         12 inches = 1 foot

            Imperial

3 feet = 1 yard   1 stone = **14** pounds

4 **(a)** Matches **D**   **(b)** Matches **B**
5 **(a) (i)**   24 inches
        (ii) 60 inches
        (iii) 18 inches
   (b) (i)   3 feet
        (ii) 4 feet 2 inches
        (iii) 5 feet
6 **(a)** 10 litres   **(b)** 30 litres

2   Algebraic expressions (pages 16–17)
1 **(a)** 14   **(b)** 0   **(c)** 20   **(d)** 7
2 **(a)** 6   **(b)** 5   **(c)** 15   **(d)** 4
3 **(a)** Cost (£) = 9 × number of CDs + 4
   (b) Cost (£) = 10 × number of CDs + 1
   (c) £40   **(d)** £51   **(e)** £3   **(f)** 3
4 **(a)** Red triangle: Perimeter = $a + a + a$, Perimeter = $3a$
        Blue triangle: Perimeter = $a + a + b$,
                       Perimeter = $2a + b$,
        Green triangle: Perimeter = $a + b + c$
                        Perimeter = $c + b + a$
   (b) (i)   Red triangle: 12 cm
                  Blue triangle: 10 cm
                  Green triangle: 9 cm
        (ii) Red triangle: 15 cm
                  Blue triangle: 13 cm
                  Green triangle: 14 cm
   (c) (i)   Yes   **(ii)** Yes
5 **(a) (i)**   126 cm²   **(ii)** 72 cm²
   (b) The surface area is found by adding together the areas of:
            two d by w rectangles
            and two d by h rectangles
            and two h by w rectangles.

3   Shape (pages 26–27)
1 **(a)** Pyramid   **(b)** Triangular prism
2 Ask your teacher to check your constructions.
3

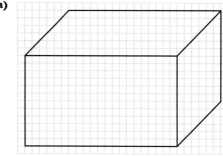

4   Data display (pages 34–35)
1 **(a)** Manager 9, Accounts 19, Secretaries 18,
          Maintenance 48,
          Cheese 32, Ham 26, Prawn 15, Salad 21
   (b) 32   **(c)** 9
2 **(a)** 4 | 00   **(b)** 157   **(c)** 585   **(d)** 428   **(e)** 23
3 **(a)** 15   **(b)** 32   **(c)** 110   **(d)** 43

5   Ratio (pages 44–45)
1 **(a)** 3 : 5   **(b)** 1 : 4   **(c)** 12
2 2 : 4 = 1 : 2   4 : 2 = 2 : 1
   3 : 9 = 1 : 3   5 : 20 = 1 : 4
3 **(a)** The money should be split in the ratio,
          boys : girls = 15 : 10 = 3 : 2. That is, 3 parts to the boys
          and 2 parts to the girls, giving 5 parts altogether.
          £50 divided by 5 = £10
          Therefore the boys get 3 × £10 = £30
   (b) The girls get 2 × £10 = £20

4

5 **(a)**

(b) Similar

6   Equations (pages 52–53)
1 **(a)** 4   **(b)** 12   **(c)** 11
   (d) 12   **(e)** 2   **(f)** 1
   (g) 20   **(h)** 3   **(i)** 2

2 **(a)** Q1 Right
         Q2 Wrong
         Q3 Right
         Q4 Right
         Q5 Wrong
         Q6 Wrong
  (b) Q2 $x = 1$
         Q5 $x = 3$
         Q6 $x = 9$

3 **(a)** Jo has 8 pencils.
  (b) Jo and Humza have 12 pencils.
  (c) Jo has twice as many pencils as Humza.

4 **(a)** 5.5 cm   **(b)** 9.7 cm   **(c)** 14.1 cm

5 **(a)** Ali's number   **(b)** 4
  (c) $3n + 7 = 40$ **(d)** 11

7 Angles and polygons (pages 60–61)

1 $a = 155$ $b = 180$ $c = 75$

2 **(a)** All the sides are equal lengths, and all the angles are equal.
  (b) (i), (iii) and (v)

3 **(a)** 30
  (b) Ask your teacher to check your construction.
  (c) Dodecahedron

4 **(a)** Irregular hexagon
  (b) a, b, e and g are acute angles
      b is an obtuse angle
      d is a right angle
      c and f are reflex angles

8 Directed numbers (pages 66–67)

1 **(a)** **(i)** 4   **(ii)** -26 **(iii)** -13
      (iv) -2 **(v)** -5 **(vi)** -25
  (b) **(i)** 4   **(ii)** -26 **(iii)** -13
      (iv) -2 **(v)** -5 **(vi)** -25

2 **(a)** 20 m **(b)** 15 m **(c)** 35 m **(d)** 5 m **(e)** 30 m

3 **(a)** £15   **(b)** $-£5$ **(c)** $-£4$

4 **(a)** **(i)** $-6\,°C$ **(ii)** $-1\,°C$ **(iii)** $+2\,°C$ **(iv)** $+1\,°C$
  (b) $7\,°C$

5 **(a)** Yes; 8 minutes   **(b)** 4 minutes slow
  (c)

Noon	Monday	Tuesday	Wednesday	Thursday	Friday
Fast or slow	Slow	Slow	Neither	Fast	Fast
How much	8 minutes	4 minutes	–	4 minutes	8 minutes

  (d) Noon on Wednesday

9 Sequences and number machines (pages 74–75)

1 **(a)** £3 + £2 = £5
  (b) Wanda: 2 × £3 + £2 = £8
      Terry: 3 × £3 + £2 = £11
  (c)

  (d)

Avonford Ice Rink						
Number of hours	1	2	3	4	5	6
Cost (including skate hire)	£5	£8	£11	£14	£17	£20

  (e) The differences are £3   **(f)** =A1*3+2

2 **(a)** +2 (for the number of pink squares)
  (b) 11   **(c)** 2   **(d)** 18   **(e)** =B1+2

10 Percentages (pages 82–83)

1 **(a)** 40%   **(b)** 4   **(c)** 20

2 **(a)** Granny got the better rate of interest. They both got the same amount of interest but Granny had less money in, so it was a higher percentage.

  (b) 6%

3

Find 10%   £6
Find 25%   £15
Increase by 10%   £66
Decrease by 25%   £45

4 **(a)** 20%
  (b) Yes: 10
      No: 22
      Don't know: 8

11 Brackets (pages 88–89)

1 **(a)** 18   **(b)** 14   **(c)** 20   **(d)** 32
  (e) 45   **(f)** 12   **(g)** 27   **(h)** 40
  (i) 19   **(j)** 76

2 **(a)** **(i)** $5 \times (2 + 4)$ **(ii)** $4 \times (4 - 2)$
      (iii) $7 \times (3 + 2)$ **(iv)** $9 \times (3 + 8 - 9)$
  (b) **(i)** 30   **(ii)** 8
      (iii) 35   **(iv)** 18

3 **(a)** 105 **(b)** 256 **(c)** 261 **(d)** 280

4 **(a)** 100 cm² **(b)** 238 cm² **(c)** 322 cm² **(d)** 612 cm²

5 **(a)** 162 **(b)** 120 **(c)** 161 **(d)** 316
  (e) 204 **(f)** 345 **(g)** 703

6 **(a)** How many rows of plants have they got altogether?
    → $20 + (25 \times 2)$
    How many plants have they got altogether?
    → $(20 \times 40) + 25 \times (40 + 55)$
    There are more plants in greenhouse 2 than in greenhouse 1. How many more? → $40 \times (25 - 20)$
    There are more rows of plants in greenhouse 3 than greenhouse 1. How many more? → $25 - 20$
  (b) **(i)** How many plants are there altogether in greenhouse 1 and 3?
      (ii) There are more plants in greenhouse 3 than greenhouse 2. How many more?

12 Fractions (pages 94–95)

1 Ask your teacher to check your table.

2 **(a)** $\frac{1}{2}$ **(b)** $\frac{1}{5}$ **(c)** $\frac{3}{4}$
  (d) $\frac{2}{3}$ **(e)** $\frac{3}{4}$ **(f)** $\frac{1}{4}$

3 Wayne: $\frac{16}{48} = \frac{1}{3}$ Andy: $\frac{12}{48} = \frac{1}{4}$ John: $\frac{20}{48} = \frac{5}{12}$

4 Jo: $\frac{1}{2} \times £60 = £30$
  Sophie: $\frac{1}{3} \times £60 = £20$
  Meena: gets £10. $\frac{10}{60} = \frac{1}{6}$

5 **(a)** $\frac{8}{8} = 1$ **(b)** $\frac{5}{5} = 1$ **(c)** $\frac{9}{9} = 1$
  (d) Any three fractions with the same numerator and denominator.

6 **(a)** $\frac{7}{11}$ **(b)** $\frac{6}{7}$ **(c)** $\frac{3}{9} = \frac{1}{3}$
  (d) $\frac{6}{8} = \frac{3}{4}$ **(e)** $\frac{8}{12} = \frac{2}{3}$ **(f)** $\frac{16}{20} = \frac{4}{5}$

7 **(a)** $\frac{1}{2} = \frac{2}{4} = \frac{4}{8}$
  (b) **(i)** $\frac{3}{4}$ **(ii)** $\frac{4}{4} = 1$ **(iii)** $\frac{2}{4} = \frac{1}{2}$
      (iv) $\frac{7}{8}$ **(v)** $\frac{3}{8}$ **(vi)** $\frac{3}{8}$

8 **(a)** **(i)** 10   **(ii)** 10   **(iii)** 10
  (b) $\frac{1}{2}$ of 100 = $\frac{1}{4}$ of 200

9 **(a)**

  (b) **(i)** $\frac{2}{12} = \frac{1}{6}$ **(ii)** $\frac{1}{2} = \frac{12}{24}$ **(iii)** $\frac{1}{4} = \frac{6}{24}$

13 Graphs (pages 102–103)

1 **(a)** JOIN THE POINTS IN ORDER
  (b) A dart.

2 (a)

x	0	2	4	6
$3x$	0	6	12	18
-3	-3	-3	-3	-3
$y = 3x - 3$	-3	3	9	15

(b)

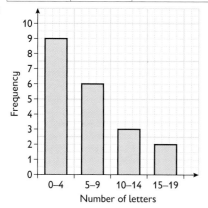

(c) $x = 1$

3 (a) (i) Up or down on the line $x = 5$.
    (ii) $(5, 8), (5, 6), (5, 5), (5, 4), (5, 3), (5, 1), (5, 0),$
    $(5, -1)$ or $(5, -2)$
(b) (i) Down one square and left or right two squares.
    (ii) $(3, 6)$ or $(7, 6)$

14 Construction and locus (pages 110–111)
1 (a) Ask your teacher to check your scale drawing.
(b) Ask your teacher to check your construction.
(c) Approximately 4.5 m
2 (a) Ask your teacher to check your construction.
(b) Ask your teacher to check your construction.
(c) They meet in the centre of the triangle.
3 (a) Ask your teacher to check your construction.
(b) Ask your teacher to check your construction.

15 Working with data (pages 118–119)
1 (a) Site A: median 45, range 36
    Site B: median 35, range 64
(b) Yes. It has the larger median and the smaller range.
2 (a)

Number of letters	Tally	Frequency
0–4	𝍩 ||||	9
5–9	𝍩 |	6
10–14	|||	3
15–19	||	2

(b)

16 Decimals (pages 126–127)
1 (a) £10.90   **(b)** £6.60   **(c)** £7.30
  (d) £8.50   **(e)** £4.70   **(f)** £16.55
2 (a) 10 **(b)** 100 **(c)** 10 **(d)** 100
  (e) 100 **(f)** 10 **(g)** 10 **(h)** 100
3 (a) 0.003, 0.0035, 0.05, 0.35, 3.5, 5.3, 35
  (b) 0.071, 0.1, 0.17, 0.7, 0.71, 7.1, 17
4

$\times$	0.2	1.5
3	0.6	4.5
8	1.6	12

$\times$	0.15	2.5
4	0.60	10
7	1.05	17.5

5 (a) 400   **(b)** 0.4   **(c)** 40   **(d)** 4
  (e) 0.04   **(f)** 0.4   **(g)** 40   **(h)** 0.4
6

Walker	Number of laps	Distance walked	Amount sponsored per km	Amount raised
Mercy	10	12.5 km	£2.00	£25
Jack	12	15 km	£4.50	£67.50

17 Algebra (pages 132–133)
1 (a) $4a$ **(b)** $2b$ **(c)** $c + 1$ **(d)** d
2 (a) $2a + 6$ **(b)** $4a + 4b$ **(c)** $6c - 9$
3 (a) $6(a + b)$ **(b)** $5(b + 2)$ **(c)** $4(2c - 3)$
4 (a) (i) 3   **(ii)** 9
  (b) (i) 15   **(ii)** 25
  (c) (i) 4   **(ii)** 0
5 (a) (i) $4a$ **(ii)** a^2
  (b) (i) $3a$ **(ii)** $15a$
6 (a) $5n + 5$
  (b) Kim: 30 sweets
    Andy: 22 sweets
    8 sweets
  (c) $4n + 6$
7 (a) Each row totals $3a$
  (b) Each column totals $3a$
  (c) Each diagonal totals $3a$
  (d) All the rows, columns and diagonals total $3a$
  (e)

4	3	8
9	5	1
2	7	6

  (f) Ask your teacher to check your answer.

18 Perimeter, area and volume (pages 140–141)
1 (a) $a = 7$ m, $b = 3$ m, $c = 12$ m, $d = 30$ m
  (b) Perimeter A = 74 m, perimeter B = 212 m
  (c) Area A = 279 m^2, Area B = 1080 m^2
2 3125 cm^3
3 12 cm^2, 20 cm^2 and 18 cm^2
4 (a) 348 cm^2 **(b)** 402 cm^2
5 4 375 000 cm^3

19 Accuracy (pages 150–151)
1

Nearest 1	1 decimal place	Nearest 10	2 decimal places
(d)	(a)	(b)	(c)
(i)	(f)	(g)	(e)
	(h)		

2 Shirts: $2 \times 11 = £22$
Chocolate bars: $9 \times 40\text{p} = £3.60$
Total = £25.60

3

Number	Rounded to nearest 1	Rounded to nearest 10	Rounded to nearest 100	Rounded to 1 decimal place	Rounded to 2 decimal places
110.178	110	110	100	110.2	110.18
84.9222	85	80	100	84.9	84.92
4506.467	4506	4510	4500	4506.5	4506.47

4

Sum	Calculator answer	Check	Checking answer	✓ or ✗
4.3 × 112	481.6	4 × 100	400	✓
99 × 42.7	4227.3	100 × 40	4000	✓
192 ÷ 11.6	16.55	200 × 10	20	✓
4341 ÷ 22	19.73	4000 ÷ 20	200	✗

5 **(a)** 60 × 2 = 120 ✓ **(b)** 300 ÷ 3 = 100 ✗
   (c) 8 × 15 = 120 ✗ **(d)** 4000 ÷ 40 = 100 ✓
6 8 × 30 = £240
   Tim pays more.

20 Real life graphs (pages 158-159)
1 **(a)** Ask your teacher to check your graph.
   (b) 10:30 **(c)** 12:45
   (d) 2 hours 15 minutes **(e)** 13 miles
2 **(a)**

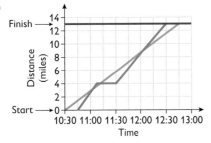

   (b) 12:10 **(c)** 3 miles
3 **(a)** **(b)** 20.8 km

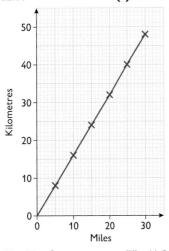

   (c) **(i)** 26 miles **(ii)** 41.6 km
4 **(a)** 550 **(b)** 11:30 **(c)** 150 **(d)** 450
5 **(a)**

   (b) 18 °C **(c)** 25 °C **(d)** 12:45

21 Working with numbers (pages 166-167)
1 **(a)** 444 **(b)** 524 **(c)** 757
2 **(a)** 46 **(b)** 212 **(c)** 89
3 **(a)** 984 **(b)** 378 **(c)** 1872
4 **(a)** 36 **(b)** 19
   (c) 22 remainder 2
5 504 fans
6 **(a)**

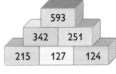

   (b)

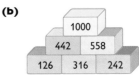

7 **(a)**

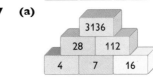

   (b)

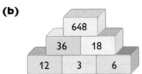

8 **(a)** **(i)** 56 **(ii)** 42
   (b) Octagonal. Saves £336

22 Transformations (pages 174-175)
1

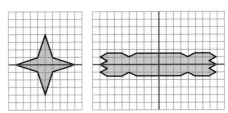

2 **(a)** 7 right **(b)** 7 left
   (c) 2 right and 4 down **(d)** 2 left and 4 up
   (e) 6 right and 4 down **(f)** 6 left and 4 up
3

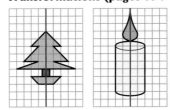

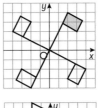

4

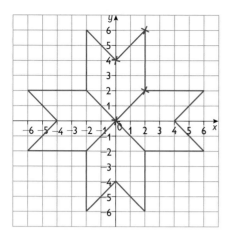

5 (a), (b), (d)

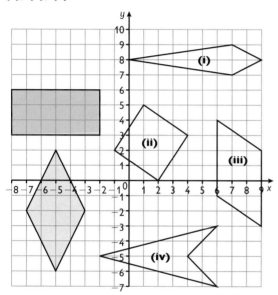

(c) (i) Kite   (ii) Square
    (iii) Parallelogram   (iv) Arrowhead
(e) Rectangle: order 2
    Rhombus: order 2
    (i) Order 1
    (ii) Order 4
    (iii) Order 2
    (iv) Order 1

6 Order 3
   3 lines of symmetry

23 Probability (pages 182–183)

1 (a) 9   (b) 3   (c) $\frac{3}{9} = \frac{1}{3}$

2 (a) $\frac{4}{20} = \frac{1}{5}$ (b) $\frac{11}{20}$ (c) $\frac{16}{20} = \frac{4}{5}$

3 (a) $\frac{11}{20}$ (b) $\frac{9}{20}$ (c) About 22

4 (a)

		Blue				
		1	**2**	**3**	**4**	**5**
Red	**1**	2	3	4	5	6
	2	3	4	5	6	7
	3	4	5	6	7	8
	4	5	6	7	8	9

(b) 20   (c) 4   (d) $\frac{4}{20} = \frac{1}{5}$ (e) $\frac{1}{20}$
(f) 5 and 6 both have a probability of $\frac{1}{5}$.